# THE TWO GREAT
# GILDERSLEEVES

## DAN MCGUIRE

The Two Great Gildersleeves
Copyright © 2020 Dan McGuire. All Rights Reserved.

No part of this book may be reproduced in any form or by any means, electronic, mechanical, digital, photocopying or recording, except for the inclusion in a review, without permission in writing from the publisher.

Published in the USA by:
BearManor Media
1317 Edgewater Dr #110
Orlando, FL 32804
www.bearmanormedia.com

Printed in the United States of America
ISBN      978-1-62933-505-6 (paperback)
          978-1-62933-506-3 (hardback)

Book and cover design by Darlene Swanson • www.van-garde.com

For Joy, Laurie, David and Jennifer,
who never cease to brighten my days.

# CONTENTS

Foreword . . . . . . . . . . . . . . . . . . . . . . . . . vii

Introduction . . . . . . . . . . . . . . . . . . . . . . . ix

The Genesis of Gildersleeve
Or: Where Did That Guy Come From? . . . . . . . . . . . 1

Peary's the Name. Not Admiral, Just Harold . . . . . . . . . 9

There's a New Gildy in Town . . . . . . . . . . . . . . . . 29

Life After Gildersleeve . . . . . . . . . . . . . . . . . . 37

Cast of Characters . . . . . . . . . . . . . . . . . . . . 43

Gildersleeve on the Big Screen . . . . . . . . . . . . . . . 79

In Conclusion . . . . . . . . . . . . . . . . . . . . . . 85

Acknowledgements . . . . . . . . . . . . . . . . . . . . 87

References . . . . . . . . . . . . . . . . . . . . . . . . 91

About the Author . . . . . . . . . . . . . . . . . . . . 93

# FOREWORD

THE SMALL-TOWN PERSONALITIES who peopled Throckmorton P. Gildersleeve's world were artfully tailored for comedic effect, though many would consider the weekly program a mellowed version of *Fibber McGee and Molly*, the situation comedy in which the character Gildersleeve originated. Few recurring characters on radio comedies were popular enough to warrant the interest of advertising agencies and the creation of a spin-off, but *The Great Gildersleeve* proved a testament to good taste as it succeeded on NBC radio for seventeen years. When he took the train from Wistful Vista to Summerfield in August of 1941, the bumptious, explosive, archetypal windbag quickly mellowed as he embraced home, work, and social life. Without an opportunity to feud with Fibber McGee, Gildersleeve traded barbs with Judge Horace Hooker, an adversary mimicking the best qualities of the *Fibber McGee and Molly* program.

The earliest episodes were focused on Gildersleeve trying to raise a niece and nephew, and balance a life of romance with women who have since been long forgotten by name except for Leila Ransom, a Southern belle who returned to the program from time to time. As the years passed, the radio scripts improved to a format unlike any other on network radio. Each contact in Summerfield deflated Gildersleeve's grandiosity and humanized him. With social lessons applied, the weekly radio broadcasts became an unlikely source of practical wisdom. The radio program made actor Harold Peary a wealthy man by the late forties. He became the star of four *Great Gildersleeve* motion pictures, along with other screen appearances in character. He made guest appearances on other radio programs as Gildersleeve. And before leaving the series, on one occasion Peary tried to purchase the rights to the radio program. With most of his income going to pay taxes, however, the price tag was too high. Kraft Foods maintained sponsorship and gave Peary another raise in salary.

In 1950, Peary jumped networks, in what is now known as the notorious talent raids, with his own program, *Honest Harold*. The CBS program was short-lived.

Willard Waterman, a friend of Harold Peary's, who could mimic the trademarked Gildersleeve laugh close enough to ensure no disappointment from listeners, was hired to replace the lead. Today, collectors of the old-time radio programs debate which of the two was better. There can never be a definitive answer. But for faithful listeners who grew up with Leroy, Marjorie, Birdie, and the rest of the gang, it was not important.

They were just happy to go along for the ride.

Dan McGuire's book is not the first written about *The Great Gildersleeve*, nor will it be the last. But Dan's book provides us with a fond look back at a bygone era when radio broadcasts brought the family together.

Martin Grams, Jr.

Martin Grams, Jr., is the editor of the bimonthly newsletter *Radio Recall*. An authority on and devoted enthusiast of old-time radio, he has written numerous books on the subject, including *The Green Hornet: A History of Radio, Comics, Motion Pictures and Television* and *The Shadow: The History and Mystery of the Radio Program, 1930-1954*. All are available on his website, *www.martingrams.biz*.

# INTRODUCTION

It was my good fortune to grow up during the peak years of what has come to be called the Golden Age of Radio. Before we were lured away by the flickering pictures on those small TV screens, a strategically located radio in the living room was a prime source of entertainment for most American families.

In most homes, that one radio served all, so the programs listened to depended on who was present. Weekdays, when Dad was at work and I was in school (or playing outside during summer vacation), Mom could go about her household chores while tuning in her favorite soap operas, quiz shows, Arthur Godfrey, or whatever. Her washing (downstairs) and vacuuming were done when there was nothing she cared to hear. She did later acquire a small Crosley radio to set atop the refrigerator so she could listen as she did kitchen chores.

Weekday afternoons, I had free access to tune in any of my favorite kids' adventure programs. Chicago's three major stations offered a widely varied selection of fifteen-minute continued series between four thirty and six o'clock. It was a tough choice to pick, and I often switched back and forth between two programs during commercials.

Weekends and evenings, Dad had first choice. He was a classical music lover, and tried to catch the live broadcasts of concerts by the New York Philharmonic, the Cleveland Symphony, the Boston Pops and others. If I was in the house, he sometimes would call me to listen when the orchestra was playing "Flight of the Bumblebee" (theme music for *The Green Hornet*) or the *William Tell* Overture. The latter was a challenge for me because it consisted of four movements. Not until the last did I get to enjoy the entirety of the theme for one of my favorite programs, *The Lone Ranger*.

Apart from his classical music programs, Dad usually deferred to Mom for evening shows. Most of her choices were comedy or musical variety programs that he also enjoyed.

I joined them for some of the comedy shows. The antics of Fanny Brice on *Baby Snooks* appealed to my juvenile sense of humor. I collected some good jokes to share with my pals by listening to *Can You Top This?* Red Skelton evoked a lot of laughs from me with his many wacky characters, especially Junior, "the mean widdle kid."

One show that I tried not to miss was *Fibber McGee and Molly*. Although some of the gags went over my head, I was fascinated by all the interesting people who dropped in to visit the folks at 79 Wistful Vista: Wallace Wimple, Abigail Uppington, Mayor LaTrivia, Mr. Old Timer and others.

Somewhere along the line, the McGees acquired new neighbors and began to have regular visits by a fellow named Throckmorton P. Gildersleeve. He was rather full of himself and a bit of a windbag. He and Fibber tended to disagree on many subjects, which resulted in frequent comical arguments that eventually had to be interrupted by the patient Molly. This came to be a part of the program that I especially looked forward to.

When Gildersleeve departed to take on a program of his own, my folks never thought it necessary to explain this to me. I contin-

## INTRODUCTION

ued to enjoy the *McGee* program, but wondered when Gildersleeve would visit again. After a while, I concluded that, for some reason, he was gone.

Then one evening I poked my head into the living room to see what my folks were listening to, and I heard a familiar voice. "Hey!" I said. "That's Mr. Gildersleeve!" Only then did the folks explain that he had left Wistful Vista to take up a new role on his own program. I sat down to listen.

The story line was quite different, but Gildersleeve was still the somewhat pompous fellow with that wicked laugh. He was surrounded by a new group of characters who were interesting and amusing in their own way. *The Great Gildersleeve* became one of my regular evening programs.

This book is a fond remembrance of "Gildy," his family and friends, and the show that helped me make the transition from kid stuff to grown-up listening in those long-ago days of old-time radio.

Dan McGuire

Harold Peary, a.k.a. Throckmorton P. Gildersleeve

# THE GENESIS OF GILDERSLEEVE OR: WHERE DID THAT GUY COME FROM?

In the beginning, Don Quinn created a small town somewhere in the heart of the U.S.A. Don looked and saw that it was good. He called the town Wistful Vista.

Don decreed that a couple named Fibber and Molly McGee should live in the town. He created a modest home for them at 79 Wistful Vista. Don looked and saw that it was good.

Don bestowed the home upon the McGees and told them to go hence and be funny. They did, and great numbers of people were amused. Don was pleased and saw that it was good.

Well, actually, it was a bit less celestial than that. Don Quinn did, indeed, create *Fibber McGee and Molly*, one of radio's most popular comedy programs, but he did so at the behest of a couple named Jim and Marian Jordan.

The Jordans were former vaudevillians who had made the transition to that new medium that was capturing the attention of people in big cities, small towns, and rural areas around the country. Their musical abilities included the piano, ukulele and guitar, in addition to beautiful singing voices. They also were skilled at doing numerous voices and dialects.

In Chicago, which boasted several large radio stations and numerous smaller ones, they found ample work on both musical and comedy programs. Early in the 1930s, they were doing quite well in spite of the Great Depression, but they worked at the whim of stations and their program directors. They yearned to have a program that they could call their own.

Their friend Don Quinn was roaming from station to station picking up work as a freelance writer. They asked if he would try to come up with something for them. Don was pleased to oblige.

Within a couple of weeks, Don had the first draft of a script. He presented it to Jim and Marian. They made some cuts and additions and gave it a practice run with Don doing some of the voices.

With the format roughly established, Don began working on a few more scripts and they started shopping the program around. Their timing proved propitious. S. C. Johnson & Company, makers of numerous Johnson's Wax products, was looking for a program on which to advertise its products. They were open to music, drama or comedy, but preferred the latter. The Jordans and Don Quinn auditioned their favorite of Don's scripts before half a dozen company executives. The response was uniform approval.

After another visit to negotiate contract details, the Johnson company bought air time on NBC and the network began an advance publicity campaign. On April 16, 1935, before a live audience in the studio of NBC's New York City station, the Jordans premiered their new show, *Fibber McGee and Molly*. Though not an instant hit, it was well received. The Jordans then returned to Chicago to air subsequent programs from the network's station WMAQ. Don Quinn gave up his freelance work and became the Jordans' full-time writer.

The format of the program was simple. As created by Quinn,

the town of Wistful Vista was big enough to have all the commercial and recreational facilities of a modest-size city, but small enough that almost everyone seemed to know everyone else. Each week the McGees would be visited by a number of townsfolk or neighbors. Their varied personalities would produce comic back-and-forth conversations.

Don Quinn proved to have one of radio's most creative comic imaginations. In his years with the Jordans, he produced more than a hundred characters who dropped in on the McGees. Many appeared just once or twice and then apparently left town when they failed to produce the desired laughs. Others proved to be so popular that they continued to pop in almost weekly, and audiences looked forward to their arrival.

The versatile Bill Thompson played a henpecked milquetoast fellow named Wallace Wimple. Ol' Wimp, as McGee called him, carried a bird book about with him and often had written a poem that just happened to be appropriate for whatever activity was going on at the McGee residence. His visits always included a sad-voiced account of some unpleasant encounter with the spouse who greatly outweighed him: "Last week, Sweetie Face—that's my big old wife…"

In a sort of tired cackle, sometimes on the same episode, Thompson would portray the character known simply as Mr. Old Timer. As he chatted with the McGees, Fibber would tell a joke that was a bit corny and not especially funny. Old Timer would chuckle politely and then say, "That's purty good, Johnny, but that ain't the way I heee-rrred it. The way I heee-rrred it, one feller says t'other feller, 'saaaaay, he says…'" The expression "That ain't the way I heee-rrred it" became a catch phrase with millions of fans and even folks who weren't regular listeners.

Isabel Randolph joined the cast as the rich and snobbish Mrs. Kuppenheim. Don Quinn had fun giving the McGees comic lines designed to bring her down a peg, but he was not happy with her name. She became Mrs. Mitchell-Twitchell, Mrs. J. Walter Loganberry, Mrs. Uppingham Upson and, finally, Mrs. Abigail Uppington. Fibber nicknamed her "Uppy" and remarked to Molly that she was obliged to use a lorgnette because her nose was so out of joint that she could not wear regular glasses.

When Isabel Randolph left the program, both Don Quinn and the Jordans missed Uppy. So Quinn invented another upper crust madam named Mrs. Millicent Carstairs. Played to perfection by Bea Benaderet, she once told the McGees that she and her husband raised navel oranges in their backyard, but lest she sound vulgar she referred to them as "citrus-umbilicus." Benaderet probably is best remembered for her later role starring on television's *Petticoat Junction*.

Gale Gordon, who would later make life miserable for Lucille Ball on her *Here's Lucy* television show, joined the program and played a few incidental characters before becoming Wistful Vista's pompous Mayor Charles LaTrivia. A seasoned actor on numerous dramatic programs, Gordon had never before attempted a comedy role. He proved to have a knack for it, and LaTrivia would prove to be one of the McGees' most popular and anticipated visitors.

While boasting of a recent mayoral accomplishment, LaTrivia would use some elaborate phrase that the McGees pretended not to understand. As he attempted to rephrase, Fibber and Molly took turns interrupting and sounding more confused.

LaTrivia: I consider myself a bit of a raconteur, and I …

McGee: A rake on tour, hey! Does that mean you gad about making merry with the single ladies of our fair town?

LaTrivia (flustered): No, no, I would never …

Molly: Of course not, McGee. I think what Mr. Mayor means is that he carries a rake with him so he can be a good neighbor and help folks rake up their leaves and gardens.

The McGees' back-and-forth interruptions led to LaTrivia getting his own words twisted and becoming increasingly flustered and irritated. Gordon proved to be a master of the slow burn. His Honor's voice began to rise as he helplessly protested: "I never said I was raking sleeves—eh, taking leaves—when I said 'rag and tour'—eh, 'tag and roor'—you're the one who—I never—you—"

At last, completely incoherent and nearly shouting, he would stop to take a long breath and calm himself as the audience roared with laughter. Then, defeated, he would mutter, "Oh, good day!" and exit to the sound of the door slamming.

A much calmer visitor was Dr. George Gamble, played by Arthur Q. Bryan. McGee would address him as "tummy thumper," "bone bender," or "serum salesman" and note that his patients were eating two apples a day in hopes of avoiding him. In contrast to LaTrivia, the good doctor would maintain his easygoing demeanor. Addressing McGee as "mental lightweight" or "Marblehead," he responded with gentle but barbed comments about Fibber's Neanderthal intellect. For all that, the two got on well enough to be frequent fishing partners.

Even announcer Harlow Wilcox apparently lived somewhere in town, for each week he popped in about midway in the show. McGee dubbed him Waxy because, invariably, something in their conversation would remind him of the shine that his kitchen floor linoleum took on when he applied a coat of Johnson's Self-Polishing Floor Wax. "There's no rubbing, no buffing," he reminded them. "Just apply and let dry." McGee would greet his arrival with a wary welcome. "What's on your mind today, Waxy? As if I didn't know."

In addition to all these "regulars," the McGees were visited by numerous others who showed up intermittently when Don Quinn needed to fill a gap in the script. In 1937, long before LaTrivia's arrival, the McGees were visited by a blustery mayor named Appleby. Fibber quickly nicknamed him Applepuss.

A *Fibber McGee* cast photo, circa 1939. From left: The King's Men quartet, orchestra leader Billy Mills, Jim and Marian Jordan, Harold Peary, Bill Thompson, Isabel Randolph, announcer Harlow Wilcox.

Played by a new cast member named Harold Peary, Appleby garnered only modest laughter and was soon gone. But Peary hung around, showing up sporadically in a number of guises: an interior decorator, a bombastic Army general, a dentist, an optometrist and a taxi driver. With appropriate voice changes, he became an Italian wrestler, the stuffy Cicero Clod and the veddy British Lord Bingham.

Peary was happy to be working regularly on the program, and he enjoyed using his vocal talents to portray a string of goofy personas. But he told Don Quinn that he would really like to have a continuing character such as Isabel Randolph's Uppy or Bill Thompson's Wimple.

Peary got his wish on the night of October 3, 1939, when he assumed a persona that was to be more enduring. Don Quinn decreed that the McGees would have new next-door neighbors. To announce their arrival, a fellow who introduced himself as Throckmorton P. Gildersleeve visited Fibber and Molly. It was to be a portentous meeting for the McGees, and even more so for Harold Peary.

Don Quinn looked and saw that it was good.

Harold Peary in an NBC promo photo

# PEARY'S THE NAME.
# NOT ADMIRAL, JUST HAROLD.

He made his initial entrance in San Leandro, California, on July 25, 1908. His parents, who were of Portuguese descent, named him Harrold Jose Pereira de Faria. They remembered that even at his birth he had strong lungs.

His name sufficed to get him through his boyhood and high school, but it had a non-native sound and was too long for marquees. It would one day need to be changed.

While still a young tyke, Harrold demonstrated an enthusiasm for singing and the ability to carry a tune. By age eleven, he was performing as a boy soprano at weddings, banquets and other events in the San Leandro area, usually for a modest fee. For friends and neighbors he might settle for a free meal and some cake to bring home to his parents.

When he was but thirteen, he was somehow "discovered" and made his radio debut on station KLX. He was billed as "The Oakland Tribune's Boy Caruso."

By the time he was seventeen, he had become a baritone and began taking singing lessons. His urge to perform led to him singing in musical comedies with several summer stock and touring companies. He did, however, complete his education, first at St. John's Academy and then at St. Mary's Highland College. Somewhere along the way, he shortened his name and Americanized what was left to Harold Perry.

While singing on San Francisco's station KZM in 1923, he caught someone's attention. He soon had his own show, *The Spanish Serenader*. In an *Oakland Tribune* review, his last name was misspelled as Peary. Harold liked it, began spelling it that way himself, and later had his name legally changed.

His stage experience and the ability to do various voices led to his first non-singing appearance on radio. In 1929, he was given an acting role on *Roads to Romance*. He also was heard on *Spotlight Revue* and did skits with cowboy singer Charlie Marshall on *Mr. Marshall and Mr. Peary*.

It was also in that year that he met and romanced an attractive lady named Wanda (Betty) Farquhar. On May 14, 1929, she became Mrs. Harold Peary.

In 1930, he spent six months working on NBC as a staff actor and singer. Various stage and radio appearances kept him busy for the next dozen years. They also kept him well fed. He developed a slight paunch that remained with him and became part of his character years later.

In 1935, Harold and Betty moved to Chicago. Harold envisioned new and more enriching opportunities in radio as it captured more and more listeners around the country. As he made himself known to local stations, he soon was singing on various musical programs. Just as frequently, he found himself doing spoken parts on a number of dramatic programs.

One of his early prize roles was on a Christmas story written by Arch Oboler for the popular creepy horror program *Lights Out*. He also was heard on *First Nighter, Grand Hotel, The Story of Mary Marlin, Girl Alone* and *Little Orphan Annie*.

A young Harold Peary

His flexible voice enabled him to play several roles on the same program. The producers loved it, because they could populate the script's characters with fewer paid actors. On some occasions, he played four or five characters on one program. On the kids' adventure series *Tom Mix Straight Shooters*, he was at times Sheriff Mike Shaw, the outlaw brothers Shotgun and Hawk Barrett, an Indian chief, even Lee Lou, the Chinese cook. He voiced eight different characters, albeit not on one episode.

In Chicago, Peary became part of what was jokingly called the "Bridge is Up" gang. Three major stations, WBBM, WGN and WMAQ, were in buildings a few blocks apart. Two were on one side of the Chicago River and one on the other. The bridge was at times raised for boats heading to Lake Michigan or returning. Freelance actors like Peary often worked ten-hour days, performing on many different programs at all three stations. If they finished one program and dashed to another station across the river, they prayed that the bridge would not be up.

Many of the busiest players bribed elevator operators to watch for them racing in the door and give them priority getting up to the studio floor. Writers for continuing drama programs sometimes helped by not having a particular character appear until several pages into the script.

In an early role that may have seemed inconsequential at the time, Peary played the Italian father of a pupil on *Kaltenmeyer's Kindergarten*. It was a nonsense comedy program in which the pupils gave silly answers to a teacher who was never really in charge. There Harold made friends with fellow cast members Jim and Marian Jordan. That friendship led to his joining the cast of *Fibber McGee and Molly* in 1937.

Early in his tenure, before Don Quinn had come up with a definitive character for him, Peary would sit in the audience during the show's "warm-up" period. When announcer Harlow Wilcox welcomed the audience and told them what show was about to start, Peary would leap up and run out yelling, "Let me out of here!"

One of his first roles on *Fibber McGee and Molly*, heard on October 4, 1937, was the blustery Mayor Appleby. In November he was heard as Wistful Vista's druggist, Mr. Cramer. In February, 1938, he morphed into a character who stuck around for awhile, the Chinese laundryman, Gooey-Fooey. Finally, on October 17, 1939, he came visiting and introduced himself as the McGees' new neighbor, Throckmorton P. Gildersleeve.

Writer Don Quinn was fond of the name Gildersleeve. On numerous previous shows he had Peary appear as many different characters with the name. Each time, he would have a different first name, none of which Don felt was quite right. While they were discussing the new character that Peary would play, Harold mentioned that he lived on Throckmorton Street. Quinn's eyes lit up and he said, "That's it!" A middle initial, P (for Peary), was added, and the two agreed it was the perfect moniker for the McGees' new overblown neighbor.

In his new persona, Gildersleeve was a bit of a windbag, pompous and opinionated. With a rather inflated regard of himself, he was prone to be argumentative when his views were questioned. Fibber, as his name implies, was given to stretching the truth to great lengths, especially when recounting tales of his own past accomplishments. His views on almost any subject were likely to be directly opposite of those expressed by the self-assured Gildersleeve. This made for many verbal disputes replete with comic insults.

Each week some minor difference of opinion would set the two off on a comic exchange of jibes involving references to low mentality and nonsensical efforts to prove a point. Gentle Molly would remain quiet until their voices began to rise. Then she would interrupt with a soft, but stern, "Boys, boys!" That would bring the debate to an end as both men apologized to Molly, but not to each other.

In a quieter voice, Fibber would then direct one last joking jab at Gildersleeve, who would respond by saying in a wounded tone,

"Oh, you're a h-a-a-a-a-a-rd man, McGee." It came to be a standard wrap-up to his visit that always got some chuckles from the audience.

On one occasion, the cast was doing an afternoon rehearsal before a live audience. Gildersleeve had a little joke that he was telling the McGees, and the script instructed him to laugh afterward. He laughed, but not just a "Ha, ha!" laugh. Instead, he improvised. Starting on a high note that sounded a bit like a giggle, he used his vocal talent to go down the scale until he reached a deep bottom note that sounded almost like a growl.

It came off sounding like the satisfied laugh of someone who has gotten away with something naughty and is the only one who knows it. The laugh itself got a laugh from the audience. After the rehearsal, the Jordans and Don Quinn all complimented Peary on it. They unanimously agreed: "Leave it in."

Leave it in, he did. It became a trademark of the Gildersleeve character. Peary referred to it as his "dirty laugh."

Gildersleeve became one of the most regular visitors to the McGee abode, and one of the most anticipated by the audience. An occasional story line expanded his role to that of featured player. On one episode, when Molly's rich ex-boyfriend comes to visit, the McGees persuade Gildersleeve to dress up and pretend to be their butler. Throckmorton fumes as McGee thinks of petty tasks for him in front of their guest.

When the Jordans prevailed upon NBC to let them transfer the program to the West Coast, most of the cast, including Peary, went with them. The last Chicago broadcast was January 24, 1939. Harold and Betty Peary were soon settled in a house in Encino, not far from the Jordans. In the Jordans' oversize backyard, the cast and crew enjoyed many barbeque parties. Harold Peary soon was being called Hal, a name he preferred.

Hal Peary does his grumpy Gildersleeve.

Proximity to Hollywood proved providential for Peary. The 1940 Paramount Pictures comedy *Comin' Round the Mountain* starred Bob Burns. Thanks to the popularity of his *McGee* character, Hal was cast as Mayor Gildersleeve.

In 1941, he appeared in *Country Fair*. He was elevated to the dubious role of a candidate for governor being promoted by the star, Eddie Foy, Jr. Though there was little resemblance to his Wistful Vista persona, he was again named Gildersleeve.

Producers of the two films may have thought that radio listeners might not know the Peary name but would come to the theaters to see Gildersleeve.

The role of Gildersleeve appeared to assure Hal a solid place in the *Fibber McGee* cast for as long as the show retained its popularity. The security was gratifying, but Hal was restless, in part because it afforded him no opportunity for his first love, singing.

As the *McGee* program neared its 1941 summer break, NBC presented him with an appealing offer.

Someone had suggested a program featuring Gildersleeve as a

summer replacement. NBC shopped the idea to the Johnson's Wax people. They didn't bite, but Kraft Foods was looking for a program on which to promote its Parkay margarine and other products. They liked the idea and would take on the program if it was a regular feature, not a summer fill-in.

NBC ran the idea past Peary, who was delighted. When assured that some singing could be worked in, he was sold.

At the outset, Jim and Marian Jordan had prudently arranged to retain all rights to their program. That made the Gildersleeve character their property. But they were good friends with Hal and happy to turn loose the character. Though money was not a prime consideration, there no doubt was some legal negotiating with NBC that involved a monetary remuneration.

Peary signed a five-year contract with both NBC and Kraft Foods. It required him to perform only on NBC and to cease using his own name. The proposed title for his program was *The Great Gildersleeve*, and he would henceforth be known by that name. It was a bit restrictive, but at the time Peary took it as a minor concession. He would from time to time be a guest on other programs and even once starred on *Lux Radio Theatre*, the highly-rated program that recreated popular films on radio.

The writers quickly went to work on an introductory script. Leonard Levinson was assigned as head writer. He had worked with Don Quinn on the *McGee* program and knew the Gildersleeve character well. An audition of the program before a live audience was gratifying, with laughs in the right places. Some fine tuning was done as NBC began promoting the forthcoming new show.

On Sunday evening, August 31, 1941, *The Great Gildersleeve* had its premiere broadcast before a live audience with a full orchestra. It laid the groundwork for all future episodes as Gildersleeve headed for the town of Summerfield to look after his recently orphaned niece and nephew, Marjorie and Leroy Forrester.

Over the summer, Throckmorton had transformed. He was now a bachelor. On the *McGee* program, he had been married. His wife never appeared, but was mentioned at times, usually to facilitate a gag about married life. Had he brought her along, she would surely have assumed a motherly role for the youngsters. Gildersleeve would not have been confronted with so many vexing problems in rearing them. It would also have precluded his many comic romances with various ladies.

So "the great man," as announcers would come to call him, was single again. *Fibber McGee* listeners may have forgotten that he was married or just accepted the change. Peary told an interviewer years later that NBC never had a letter from anyone asking what happened to Gildersleeve's wife.

On the overnight train to Summerfield, Throckmorton had the misfortune to be seated in the diner with a rather cranky sourpuss named Horace Hooker (Earle Ross). Conversation between the two opinionated men proved less than amiable, with insults being passed both ways across the table, including references to Gildersleeve's girth. At bedtime, he found that he was in the berth above Hooker, who snored loudly. Unable to sleep, he poured a cup of cold water on the offender.

Only later did he learn that his disagreeable dinner companion was Judge Hooker, who sat the bench in Summerfield's court. If Gildersleeve was to assume guardianship of his niece and nephew, he would need to meet the stringent requirements of the stern and sharp-tongued judge.

The judge did not make it easy. Gildersleeve had to endure some ornery judgmental criticisms, but eventually won grudging approval. The judge's sharp eye—and tongue—were directed at Gildersleeve for some time.

As Gildersleeve settled in, listeners met the other members of the household. Marjorie (Lurene Tuttle) was about seventeen, with a young girl's propensity for brief infatuations with various boys. She was a good student and mostly levelheaded. Early on, she addressed Gildersleeve as Uncle Throckmorton, but eventually shortened that to Uncle Mort, and later, Unkie.

Leroy (Walter Tetley) was an indefinite ten or eleven, and would remain so for most of the program's duration. It was he who initially called Gildersleeve Uncle Mort. He soon reduced that to Unk. He was mostly well-behaved, but a young boy's penchant for mischief sometimes got him into trouble that required Gildersleeve's fumbling efforts to get him out. He would try to make excuses, saying, "But, gee whiz, Unk…," which prompted his uncle to cut him off with a deep-voiced "Leee-roy!" Nonetheless, Gildersleeve would acquire an affection for the lad that at times prompted what became a catch phrase: "You're a briiii-ight boy, Leroy!"

Perhaps to remind listeners of Gildersleeve's origin, a pre-Christmas episode has him shopping at the local bargain basement and purchasing a gift to send to his former neighbor, Fibber McGee. But then a very large package arrives from Wistful Vista with a "Do Not Open Until Christmas" tag. Now flustered and embarrassed, Throckmorton scurries about in search of a more appropriate (and less cheap) gift. When the mystery package is finally unwrapped, Fibber's "gift" turns out to be Gildersleeve's lawn mower, which McGee borrowed three years ago.

Part of Gildersleeve's baggage from Wistful Vista was that he arrived in Summerfield as president of Gildersleeve Girdle Works. The company motto was "If you want a better corset, of course, it's a Gildersleeve." The initial program had Gildersleeve boarding the train, bidding goodbye to assembled employees, and admonishing them to "uphold Gildersleeve girdles to the best of your ability while I'm away."

Upon learning what was the foundation of his uncle's income, Leroy uttered what was to become one of his pet phrases: "For corn's sake!" The writers initially had a little fun with girdle gags, but rather than rely on belly laughs they soon found another occupation for Gildersleeve. It was a bit of a stretch, but on October 18, 1942, he somehow got himself appointed as water commissioner of Summerfield.

Presumably, he then sold off the girdle business, though listeners were never really informed. With no real qualifications for his new position, he mostly lounged in his office while his secretary and the pump house supervisor took care of any problems that arose.

Gloria Holliday and Hal Peary

(A gossipy aside: In 1946, Peary's wife, Betty, filed for divorce. The new water department secretary on *Gildersleeve* was played by a recent addition to the cast, Gloria Holliday. A behind-the-scenes romance developed between her and Peary. While Peary's divorce was being processed, they could not marry in the United States. On August 8, 1946, during a trip to Tijuana, they had a quickie Mexican marriage. Gloria gave birth to their son, Page, on March 9, 1947. On June 24, 1947, four days after Hal's divorce was finalized, he and Gloria took their vows again in a U.S. wedding.)

Prior to Gildersleeve's arrival at the Forrester home, his wards were being cared for by the black cook and housekeeper, Birdie Lee Coggins (Lillian Randolph). A fixture in the homestead, Birdie had her own room upstairs. Having been around since Marjorie and Leroy were little ones, she served as a substitute mother figure. She was protective but not afraid to gently correct or rebuke. Nor was she reluctant to voice her opinion, respectfully, about goings-on in the household. Birdie would at times offer advice that saved the day for Gildersleeve or one of his wards. She had an infectious laugh, and when the spirit moved her, she sometimes burst into song.

That aspect of her character was a joy to Hal Peary, who also prevailed upon the writers to put his fine baritone to use in many episodes. On one show, the Summerfield Little Theatre League put on a musical called *Deep in the Heart of Maryland*.

Gildersleeve played Uncle Rufus and Birdie was his wife, Freesia. Together, they gave a rousing rendition of "What You Gonna Do When the Rent Comes 'Round?"

Within the newly reformatted family, no mention ever was made of how the elder Forresters died. Nor did Marjorie or Leroy ever mention them or voice any sadness at their absence. Gildersleeve might understandably have avoided speaking about his late sister in deference to the feelings of his wards. Yet it would seem only natural that the youngsters would at times express some feelings of loss and grief.

Lillian Randolph as Birdie Lee Coggins

The most likely explanation is that *Gildersleeve* was a comedy program. Unlike later television shows such as *All in the Family*, radio series seldom mixed humor with more serious topics. *Gildersleeve's* writers specialized in comedy and may not have felt comfortable attempting to incorporate any somber discussions into the script. Instead, they focused on the humorous, if sometimes awkward, adjustments made by Gildersleeve as he assumed his new role, and by his wards in accepting him as their new head of household.

New characters were introduced quickly. Gildersleeve soon got to know Floyd Munson (Arthur Q. Bryan), the local barber. Although married but once, he referred to his missus as "my present wife." His reputation for gossip led Gildersleeve to remark, "Telling Floyd anything is like placing a full-page ad in the town newspaper."

Peavey's Drugstore was owned and operated by the soft-spoken Richard Quincy Peavey (Richard LeGrand). It seemed he seldom sold any drugstore items, but he frequently moved to the soda fountain to serve someone one of his meticulously prepared sodas or sundaes.

Both Gildersleeve and Leroy visited him frequently when they had some problem to resolve. His mild-mannered persona made him a nonjudgmental sounding board.

For Gildersleeve, though, it was always a frustrating consultation. He would expound upon some perplexing situation and then conclude with his judgment as to what should be done. Peavey then would softly respond, "Well, now, I wouldn't say that." Which led the exasperated Gildersleeve to demand, "Well, then, what *would* you say?"

At Floyd's barbershop, Throckmorton became acquainted with Summerfield's police chief, Donald Gates (Ken Christy). Almost as mild-mannered as Peavey, he seemed ill-suited for his position. Fortunately, Summerfield's most serious crimes involved traffic violations.

Once Gildersleeve proved his worthiness to become guardian to Marjorie and Leroy, Judge Hooker softened a bit. He took to calling Throckmorton "Gildy." They assumed a guarded friendship that did not preclude frequent ribbing of each other. The judge especially liked to poke fun at Gildy's girth. When he got off what he thought was a clever jab, he had a kind of billy goat laugh. Gildy would respond with an annoyed "Omph!" Under his breath, he would mutter, "You old goat!"

A cast photo, circa 1949. Front row, from left: Lillian Randolph, Gloria Holliday, Una Merkel, Mary Lee Robb. Back row: Earle Ross, Richard LeGrand, Walter Tetley, Hal Peary, Jack Meakin (music director), John Wald (announcer), Arthur Q. Bryan.

Nevertheless, Gildersleeve and Hooker were soon to join the others in a little fellowship group. It seemed Floyd had an old upright piano in a room above the barbershop. He and the others formed a group they called the Jolly Boys Club. In their loose fellowship, most members picked up on Hooker's calling Gildersleeve Gildy. The ever-polite Peavey was the exception, mostly addressing him as Mr. Gildersleeve.

The club was a generally convivial gathering, and members often offered one another sage advice on various problems, but most of all its purpose was singing. Floyd played the piano. With his fine baritone, Gildy took the lead. The chief's deep bass provided the background. In spite of an occasional sour note, the others managed a passable harmony. The evening would start with the Jolly Boys' theme:

"Oh, it's always fair weather,

When good friends get together…"

Peavey was fond of the song "There's a Tavern in the Town." He frequently suggested that the group lend their voices to it, but he usually was outvoted or simply ignored.

Occasionally, an overheated debate or off-key performance would lead to some bickering. Chief Gates would then be the peacemaker, remonstrating: "Fel-las, fel-las! Let's all be Jolly Boys!"

Hal Peary especially enjoyed this part of the show. It was incorporated in many scripts and afforded him the chance to put his singing voice to work. In addition to his participation with the group, he sang many solos.

*The Great Gildersleeve* was a transition from *Fibber McGee and Molly* in more ways than one. The *McGee* format usually had some thin story line such as Fibber needing glasses or Molly wanting a lamp repaired. That would be the background story as they received various visitors and would be resolved by show's end. Seldom did a plot carry over to the next week.

By contrast, *Gildersleeve* had continuing story lines—sometimes more than one—that carried over for many weeks. Each weekly program had a beginning and ending that could be enjoyed as a stand-alone episode. But the overarching story line continued and helped to bring listeners back each week.

A family budget planning session: Hal Peary (Gildersleeve) surrounded by Lurene Tuttle (Marjorie), Lillian Randolph (Birdie) and Walter Tetley (Leroy).

A prevailing theme was the great man's perception of himself as a ladies' man. This resulted in numerous encounters with ladies hard to get and others out to get him. The first of these was the widow Leila Ransom (Shirley Mitchell), who moved into the vacant house next door. The Savannah native portrayed herself as a genuine Southern belle and saw Gildy as an excellent catch. She responded warmly to his flirting and was given to such utterances as "Mercy, me," "Do be a lamb" and "Oh, Throck-mor-ton, you are sooo ro-man-tic!"

She was around for much of the 1942 season. She flitted—or flirted—in and out of the script as other things were happening week to week. Gildersleeve proposed and the two actually made it to the altar. But her long-missing husband, who had been presumed dead, burst in just in time to respond to the preacher's question as to whether anyone knew any reason, etc.

Adeline Fairchild (Una Merkel) enticed Gildy with a less overdone Southern charm. The writers had fun with a little inside joke when one of Gildersleeve's pals remarked that she looked like Ingrid Bergman. Gildy replied, "She looks more like Una Merkel to me."

Other ladies who attracted Gildy's eye included Leroy's school principal, Eve Goodwin (Bea Benaderet). When Leroy got wind of that, it prompted another of his pet expressions: "What a character!" Leroy did, however, come to admire his uncle a bit more when he became an air raid warden during World War II.

Kathryn Milford (Cathy Lewis) was a nurse at Summerfield Hospital. When she mentioned that she liked to samba, Gildy signed up for dance lessons.

So it went. The incurably romantic Gildersleeve met and wooed dozens of lovely ladies and became engaged to several. In one comedy of errors, he found himself engaged to two women at the same time. He approached the altar numerous times, but each time fate—and the writers—pulled him back from the brink.

By 1944, the program and Gildersleeve were popular enough that Capitol Records signed Hal to do a series of albums for children. They were titled *Stories for Children—Told in His Own Way by the Great Gildersleeve*. With orchestral background, Hal used multiple voices to tell the stories of *Rumpelstiltskin*, *Puss in Boots*, and *Jack and the Beanstalk*. At the end of each disc, Peary spoke directly to the kiddies, telling them: "Turn the record over now; I'll wait," and "Go change the record while I light a cigar."

The first album sold well, and in 1946 he recorded the tales of *The Brave Little Tailor* and *Hansel and Gretel*. The final album, released in 1947, contained the stories of *Cinderella* and *Snow White and Rose Red*. For good measure, Peary and Capitol teamed up again in 1949. This time, in a somewhat different genre, Hal enacted the Dr. Seuss story of *Gerald McBoing-Boing*.

One of the program's most memorable continued stories began with the first episode of the 1948-1949 season. Gildy goes shopping and returns to his car to find a baby girl wrapped up in blankets lying on the front seat of his car. His search for the infant's parents is futile, so he brings her home. In the weeks that follow, as a wider search ensues, the family becomes attached to the little girl. Gildy contemplates adoption, but Judge Hooker tells him he will need to be married. On the Christmas Eve episode, the infant's father comes to claim her and explains the poignant circumstances that led him to leave the infant in the car that he knew belonged to Gildersleeve.

Kraft Foods took advantage of the story to run a contest, inviting listeners to suggest a name for the baby. Four new Ford cars were awarded to those whose entries were deemed the best. It was a good way to get a measure of listenership, which appeared to be quite favorable.

It continued thus into the 1950s, but somewhere along the way Hal Peary had become restless. He longed for a format that would involve more singing. He also was frustrated that NBC curtailed his appearances on other programs where he might make use of his talent for multiple voices and dialects.

In the late 1940s, CBS was making an infamous raid upon other networks with tempting offers to draw away top talent. Jack Benny, Red Skelton, Bing Crosby and others had made the switch. During the 1949-1950 season, Peary joined the exodus and signed with CBS. He then belatedly asked Kraft Foods to come along and continue sponsoring the *Gildersleeve* show there.

To his dismay, they declined. The Kraft people told him they had a good working relationship with NBC. Notwithstanding the *Gildersleeve* program's popularity, they chose not to switch networks. Peary's CBS contract forbade him from appearing on NBC. Regrettably, his days as *The Great Gildersleeve* were over.

Fearful that their highly regarded program might die, Kraft consulted with NBC. They were told not to worry. A fellow named Willard Waterman was waiting in the wings.

# THERE'S A NEW GILDY IN TOWN

IN THE SUMMER before he began college, Willard Lewis Waterman was attracted to a theatrical group in Madison, Wisconsin, and talked his way into a small role in their production of *The Drunkard*. Enrolled during the mid-1930s at the University of Wisconsin to study engineering, he began skipping those classes to attend a drama class. He joined Theta Chi and acted in several plays. He also spent several hours a day announcing and playing records on WHA, the university radio station.

As Waterman tells it, he decided this was much more fun than engineering and his original career choice was abandoned. He found his first modestly paying radio job at Madison's station WIBA, where he sang in a quartet that did musical interludes between programs.

Early in 1936, he moved to Chicago and was hired by NBC, where he was given small parts on several programs at station WMAQ. Later that year, he replaced the departing Harold Peary and played several of Peary's roles on the *Tom Mix Straight Shooters* program. The two struck up what would be a lifelong friendship.

Like Peary, Waterman was able to modify his voice and do numerous dialects. Producers were pleased to have him play two or more parts on one program because he received the same fee regardless. In 1937, he was a founding member of the American Federation of Radio Artists, which later evolved into the American Federation of Television and Radio Artists (AFTRA). The union's efforts effected a new rule that actors playing two or more roles were paid for each.

Willard Waterman, the new Gildersleeve

Willard's contract with NBC made him an as-needed performer on various programs, but did not restrict him from performing on other stations. He was heard on *Chandu the Magician* and *The Whistler*. He soon became a regular or frequently recurring character on such daytime shows as *The Romance of Helen Trent*, *Road of Life*, *Ma Perkins*, *Today's Children* and *The Guiding Light*, where he was a lead character.

With his versatility of voice and dialect, he played many roles on *Fifth Row Center*, *Grand Hotel*, *Knickerbocker Playhouse* and *First Nighter*, evening programs that each week presented an original play, most frequently a comedy or light romance. *First Nighter* was an especially popular show, originally starring Don Ameche and June Meredith. When they moved on, the show became a showcase for the talents of Olan Soule and Barbara Luddy. Waterman was there from the beginning and became a regular in the cast. He once noted that in its annual Christmas program he had played every part over the years except that of Mary.

Performing on various Chicago stations from mornings until late evenings, Waterman was putting in forty hours or more weekly. He nonetheless found time to court a lady named Mary Anna Theleen. In 1937, she said "yes" and they married.

Besides doing well financially, Willard was enjoying himself immensely. One program proved to be a turning point for him.

On *That Brewster Boy*, which later morphed into *Those Websters*, he and Constance Crowder played the parents of the precocious young Joey. The show centered on the trouble that Joey and his pals got into and out of. Joey was played for a time by Arnold Stang, who went on to work with Milton Berle and Henry Morgan, and later by Dick York, who would one day become Darrin Stephens on the popular television show *Bewitched*.

In 1946, the show was moved to Los Angeles. Willard and Mary had been contemplating a move to the West Coast. This was opportunity knocking. They packed their bags and tagged along.

Once there, Waterman did not need to go searching for work. His socializing with other performers led to calls for parts on *Screen Guild Players* and *Lux Radio Theatre*. He appeared on *My Friend Irma* and *Damon Runyon Theatre*. He even played incidental black characters on *Amos 'n' Andy*. In 1947, he made the first of several secondary appearances with his friend Hal Peary on *The Great Gildersleeve*. He and Shirley Mitchell (Leila Ransom on *Gildersleeve*) worked together on the 1949-1950 season of *Leave It to Joan*, starring Joan Davis.

The summer of 1950, Willard was working steadily and enjoying the warm climate when NBC approached him with a surprise invitation. Hal Peary had gone over to CBS and was no longer available to play Gildersleeve. Would Waterman be willing to take on the role? As a friend of Hal's, and having heard the circumstances of his departure, Willard was hesitant. But he knew that Hal was not coming back, and he had no doubt he could fill the role. After some consideration, he accepted.

Having made a few incidental appearances on the program, Waterman was familiar with the story line and the character he was to play, so he had no qualms about stepping in. His voice was very similar to Peary's. When he took over the role, some listeners with keen hearing no doubt noticed the change. Others may not have picked up on it or simply paid no mind. Most listeners seldom listened to a program's closing credits. Whatever the case, NBC was not swamped with letters from people asking, "What happened to the old Gildersleeve?"

Willard was able to replicate the familiar Gildersleeve "Heh, heh, heh, heh!" chuckle. But he would not attempt to duplicate Peary's trademark "dirty laugh," partly because he might not do it as well, but mostly because Peary had invented it, and he felt it belonged to Peary.

Willard Waterman (Gildersleeve) with Mary Lee Robb (Marjorie) and Walter Tetley (Leroy)

The characters and comedy changed little. Prior to Peary's departure, Marjorie had added a few years, completed high school and had a series of short-lived romances. During Peary's last year, she met and became engaged to a fellow named Walter "Bronco" Thompson, played by Richard Crenna.

The upcoming marriage was promoted in advance in the press, on the program, and in announcer plugs on other programs. For the on-air performance, before a live audience, the cast dressed their parts. Gildersleeve donned a tuxedo to give the bride away. Judge Hooker was best man. Marjorie wore a beautiful white wedding gown. The audience loved it.

A photographer from *Look* magazine recorded the event, and additional photos were staged at a nearby Episcopal church. The magazine ran a five-page spread titled "Gildersleeve Gives the Bride Away."

The newlyweds moved into the house next door. After a respectable interval (in case listeners were counting) Marjorie gave birth—to twins! When the new parents would not allow Uncle Leroy to babysit, he complained, "Gosh, Unk, you'd think they owned those twins or something!" Kraft used the occasion of the new arrivals to hold a "Name the Twins" contest. It resulted in the newcomers being named Ronald Lynn and Ronda Linda.

Other than that, things went on much as usual at the Forrester household as Waterman assumed his role. Leroy appeared to have belatedly aged a year or two. He became interested in girls and began taking them to Peavey's drugstore to treat them to a soda or sundae. When not fraternizing with the Jolly Boys, Gildy continued to have various comical troubles, often involving some woman with whom he was smitten.

During the early 1950s, as television's picture quality and content improved, its impact upon radio programming was debilitating. *The Great Gildersleeve* was not immune. During the 1952-1953 season, many characters, including Judge Hooker, Floyd Munson, even Marjorie and Bronco, were absent on many episodes. A few new characters were introduced briefly, but did not last.

In 1954, the show's format was changed from a half hour to 15-minute episodes aired five times a week. A continuing story line was used, but the only characters heard on a regular basis were Gildersleeve, Leroy and Birdie. Gone were the studio audience and live orchestra.

In 1955, as the 15-minute radio series continued, NBC attempted to adapt the show to television. Waterman played Gildy. Walter Tetley was too old to play Leroy; that role went to a lad named Ronald Keith. Even with Birdie, Leila Ransom, Judge Hooker, Peavey and Floyd Munson back as regulars, the show lasted but thirty-nine weeks.

In a 1971 interview with old-time radio broadcaster Chuck Schaden, Harold Peary observed that part of the TV show's failure owed to viewers' seeing Gildy. He was no longer the portly fellow most radio listeners envisioned—and many had seen in one or more films. As Peary explained, Gildersleeve "was a little man who thought he was a big man." Peary's friend Waterman "did a very good job on the radio [but] he was miscast on television." At six foot four, he was not the portly fellow radio listeners envisioned. When he took Leroy to task, he was far too imposing to be humorous.

Despite the failed television effort, the show returned on radio in the fall of 1955, reduced to twenty-five minutes once a week. Listener numbers were down, but many stayed tuned; enough that after the summer break the show resumed on September 6, 1955. But the handwriting was on the studio wall. Some of the final season's shows were repeats, and it was an abbreviated season. On March 21, 1957, with faithful Birdie still watching over the household, the last episode was aired.

Offstage, Leroy was heard to moan, "Well, gee whiz, Unk!"

# LIFE AFTER GILDERSLEEVE

HAROLD PEARY'S DECISION to seek greener pastures at CBS proved to be a strategy gone painfully awry. Kraft Foods, sponsor of *The Great Gildersleeve,* chose not to leave NBC. That left him with no show for the coming season at his new home.

CBS had too much invested in Peary to let that happen. Working together with Peary, its writers quickly came up with a program called *Honest Harold.* Peary played a radio personality named Harold Hemp who hosted a homemaker's program. Harold lived with his mother, was raising an orphaned nephew, and had an assortment of goofy pals. Part of the show's shtick was that it involved what may have been a first: a radio program within a program.

The cast boasted such seasoned players as Parley Baer, Shirley Mitchell, Joseph Kearns, Mary Jane Croft and Olan Soule. Peary's wife, Gloria, came along as the radio station's switchboard operator. Peary's input in the scripting enabled him to work in an occasional opportunity to sing.

CBS was unable to round up a sponsor, so the show aired on a sustaining basis. It premiered on September 17, 1950, and lasted but one season. It was not lacking for comic situations, including Harold's multiple romances, but it lacked the warmth of

*Gildersleeve*. Some reviewers pegged it as a poor man's substitute for that show, and listeners may have agreed.

Though downcast at the show's failure, Peary determined to carry on. Perhaps to signify a new stage in his life, he shaved his moustache and lost fifty pounds. Once again able to identify as Harold (or Hal) Peary, he appeared on such popular shows as *Stars Over Hollywood* and *The Railroad Hour*. It was gratifying to again put to use his fine singing voice.

In 1954, he moved to New York for a short stint as a disc jockey on station WMGM. That was sort of fun, so when he returned to the West Coast he took up a similar slot for a year at station KABC.

He signed on as a representative for Gibraltar Savings Bank and for many years appeared in their radio and television commercials, as well as print advertising.

His second marriage, which produced a son named Page, ended in 1956 when his wife, Gloria, filed for divorce.

As the death knell sounded for comedy and drama on radio, Peary did as many others did and began working on television. In guest appearances or recurring roles he was seen on *That Girl, The Doris Day Show, Petticoat Junction, Schlitz Playhouse of Stars, The Spike Jones Show, The Addams Family, My Three Sons, The Brady Bunch, The Dick Van Dyke Show* and others. He was June Havoc's boss on her comedy series *Willy,* and played neighbor Herb Woodley on the *Blondie* television series.

For a time, he emceed a program on KCOP-TV called *Waltz Varieties*. He got a kick out of being on *Perry Mason*, where he turned out to be the murderer. On the short-lived attempt to bring *Fibber McGee and Molly* to television, he took on Gale Gordon's old role as Mayor LaTrivia.

He enjoyed doing many voices for the cartoon characters of

Hanna-Barbera and others. He supplied the voice for Red Goose Shoes commercials and many others on both radio and television.

Peary was still finding sporadic roles into the 1970s. But he had made some good investments in his early years and was quite well off financially. In 1964, he had met and married Callie Juanita Parker. The couple planned to retire and move to Hawaii in 1977. Sadly, Callie became ill that year and died in December.

Thereafter, Peary was little heard from, and in 1981 he announced that he was officially retired. He lived quietly for the next few years and died of a heart attack on March 30, 1985, at the age of seventy-six.

Even as he filled the Gildersleeve role, Willard Waterman continued to appear on other programs as the opportunity arose. He had a recurring role as Mr. Merriweather in the highly regarded but short-lived series *The Halls of Ivy*, starring Ronald Colman and his wife, Benita Hume.

Like many radio performers, he adapted to television as its screens grew larger and program quality improved. During the mid to late 1950s, he appeared in incidental or recurring roles on *My Favorite Martian, Lawman, The Eve Arden Show, Mister Ed, 77 Sunset Strip, Wagon Train, The Dick Van Dyke Show, F Troop, Laramie, General Electric Theater, Bat Masterson, The Real McCoys, Bonanza, December Bride, Cheyenne, The Joey Bishop Show*, and *Guestward, Ho!* On the *Dennis the Menace* series, he played the lovable grocer, Mr. Quigley.

In 1958, he took to the stage to play the snobbish Claude Upson in *Auntie Mame* opposite Eve Arden. During 1963-1964, he joined the cast of a touring company in *How to Succeed in Business Without Really Trying*. While the show was in Chicago, he received a backstage visit from his old friend Hal Peary. In 1966, he appeared with Angela Lansbury in the Broadway musical version of *Mame*. It ran for 1,508 performances in New York and then 443 in London. He and Angela reunited for a 1983 Broadway revival.

He had a leading role in a 1973 Broadway revival of *The Pajama Game*. In a 1978 dinner theater production, he played Mayor Shinn in *The Music Man,* and later was in a touring company production of *Kiss Me, Kate*.

Back in 1946, Waterman took advantage of his relocation to Hollywood by finding his way into dozens of films, albeit in many small supporting roles. He was again Claude Upson in the 1958 film version of *Auntie Mame* with Rosalind Russell. In *The Apartment* (1960), he played Mr. Vanderhoff, one of the men using Jack Lemmon's apartment for liaisons. Between 1949 and 1972, he appeared in more than three dozen films.

Like many film and television performers, he also found time to augment his income with the relatively undemanding role of pitchman for various products. He was seen in commercials for Alka-Seltzer, New York Life Insurance, Florsheim Shoes, Kellogg's cereals and others. By the late 1970s, Waterman was unofficially retired, but in 1980 he did a "Boss and Peterson" radio commercial for Sony. It won a Clio Award, voted the year's best commercial in its category.

Other than that, he and Mary, his wife of many years, lived a quiet life as retired seniors in their San Fernando Valley home. Willard did a lot of reading and enjoyed an occasional round of golf. He graciously accepted many invitations to appear at old-time radio conventions.

Waterman contracted bone marrow disease and died at home on February 2, 1995. He was eighty years old. He was survived by Mary and their two daughters, Lynne and Susan.

# CAST OF CHARACTERS

IN ADDITION TO its two stars, the cast of *The Great Gildersleeve* included a number of supporting players who were heard on many other programs in a wide range of roles. What follows is but selective highlights in the careers of people who played some of the program's most memorable characters.

## BEA BENADERET (EVE GOODWIN)

Beatrice "Bea" Benaderet merits a book of her own for her remarkable career. Her radio and television appearances totaled more than a thousand, earning her the nickname "Busy Bea."

She was born April 4, 1906, in New York City, but her family moved to San Francisco when she was five years old. As a young girl, she took voice and piano lessons. When just twelve years old, she performed in a school production of *The Beggar's Opera*. The manager of station KGO heard her and signed her as a vocalist. She made her formal stage debut at sixteen in a production of *The Prince of Pilsen*.

She studied at an acting school, where she perfected a number of dialects, including French, Spanish and Yiddish. That led to several roles with The Players' Guild, a San Francisco stock company. In 1926, she joined the staff of station KFRC, where she multitasked as actress, singer, writer and producer. She gained attention as a female announcer, a rarity in early radio.

Benaderet moved to Los Angeles in 1936 when she was hired by station KHJ. There she made her network debut when Orson Welles added her to his acclaimed Mercury Theatre players on *The Campbell Playhouse*.

Though it was unplanned, she switched from drama to comedy when Jack Benny called on her for a small part on his popular radio program. She played a Brooklyn-accented NBC switchboard operator, Gertrude Gearshift. When Benny wanted to make a call, she was busy gabbing with her cohort, Mabel Flapsaddle (Sara Berner). As was usually the case on the show, their gags were mostly at Benny's expense. Meant to be a one-time appearance, the routine drew so many laughs that Jack continued to be annoyed by the two gossipy operators for years.

Benaderet found that she really enjoyed comedy and was pleased to take on the role of Lucille Ball's friend Iris Atterbury on *My Favorite Husband*, a radio precursor to television's *I Love Lucy*. She became the uppity Millicent Carstairs on *Fibber McGee and Molly*, Gloria the maid on *The Adventures of Ozzie and Harriet*, and Judy's mother on *A Date with Judy*. She was Martha Granby on *Granby's Green Acres* and played a landlady on both *A Day in the Life of Dennis Day* and on *The Adventures of Maisie*, starring Ann Sothern. At one time she was appearing regularly on five shows daily.

On the *Burns and Allen* show, she was Gracie's pal, Blanche Morton, on both the radio show and the later television version. Twice nominated for an Emmy for Best Supporting Actress, she was the only supporting player on the TV show to appear throughout its eight-year run. Her husband was played by four different actors.

In 1943, she began providing most of the female voices for

characters in the Warner Bros. Looney Tunes cartoons. She was never credited because of a stipulation in Warner's contract with Mel Blanc, who did almost every male voice except Elmer Fudd. Viewers did later get to see her name as the voice of Betty Rubble on the popular TV cartoon series *The Flintstones*.

On television, Bea attained her first long overdue star billing as a result of her supporting role as Cousin Pearl Bodine on the surprise hit show *The Beverly Hillbillies*. She had hoped to play Granny, but was deemed too young and too buxom for that part. Writer Paul Henning nonetheless saw her potential for bigger things. He crafted the 1963 sitcom *Petticoat Junction* around Bea.

She played Kate Bradley, the widowed proprietress of the Shady Rest Hotel. It was a return to mostly dramatic acting, as her character was good-humored but not especially funny. The show was an immediate hit, peaking at fourth in the Nielsen ratings, and it remained in the top thirty during Benaderet's four full seasons.

After the show premiered, a routine checkup had discovered a spot on Bea's lung. It later was no longer visible, but in 1967 it reappeared. Exploratory surgery found a tumor too large to be removed. She underwent laser radiation treatment, which was deemed successful early in 1968. While she recuperated, her character was said to be on a trip.

She returned to finish the fifth season with an episode called "Kate's Homecoming." But when the sixth season began, she experienced extreme fatigue. Hospitalized again, it was found that the cancer had returned. The fourth episode of the season featured only her voice with a stand-in seen from behind.

On October 13, 1968, she died of lung cancer and pneumonia. She was sixty-two.

## ARTHUR Q. BRYAN (FLOYD MUNSON)

Born in Brooklyn, New York, on May 8, 1899, Arthur Q. (Quirk) Bryan got his start in radio in its early, formative years. In 1924, he began singing as a tenor, usually as part of a quartet. In 1929, he was tapped to fill in for a sick announcer on New York City's station WOR. He remained there in that capacity until late 1931, when he moved to Philadelphia and station WCAU. There he multitasked as writer, producer and sometime actor. Two years later, still in Philly, he was announcing at WIP. Then, whether homesick or lured by a higher salary, he was back in NYC on WHN in 1934.

In 1936, he moved to Hollywood. His writing work at WCAU apparently gained him entry at Paramount Pictures, where he became a writer, working on script scenarios. In 1938-1939, he began appearing regularly on a popular CBS Pacific Network radio program called *The Grouch Club*. That may have been what got him noticed enough that he was featured in some short-subject films.

Early in the 1940s, Bryan was featured on a CBS program called *Al Pearce and His Gang* playing a character named Waymond Wadcliffe. The name drew upon the exaggerated lisp that he used in the part.

He achieved his first and only starring role in 1942. On the NBC series *Major Hoople*, based on the popular "Our Boarding House" comic strip, he played the major opposite Patsy Moran as his wife, Martha.

Bryan's trademark skill using a lisping voice became familiar to millions when Warner Bros. put it to use in their Looney Tunes cartoons. The determined hunter Elmer Fudd was forever frustrated and outsmarted by "that wascally wabbit," Bugs Bunny. Because of Mel Blanc's contract with Warners, Arthur was never credited, but he didn't mind. He and Mel became good friends.

Though not cut out to be a leading man, Bryan appeared in several dozen films over the years. In some cameo roles, you needed to look quickly to see him, but in others he was a supporting player, albeit a minor one. He can be seen in *Samson and Delilah*, in two of the Bob Hope/Bing Crosby "Road" pictures, and in the Ozzie and Harriet film *Here Come the Nelsons*. He also was in a number of live-action shorts for Warner Bros. and Columbia Pictures.

Early in the *Gildersleeve* radio series, he played a lisping fellow named Lucius Llewellyn, but the writers soon found a better use for him as barber Floyd Munson. The Jordans were looking for someone to replace departing Gale Gordon on *Fibber McGee and Molly*, and Don Quinn created the role of Doc Gamble for Bryan. Everyone agreed that it was good.

Elsewhere, Arthur took on some supporting radio roles. He was Duke on *Forever Ernest,* Mr. Fuddle on *Blondie* and Lt. Levinson on *Richard Diamond, Private Detective*, with Dick Powell.

Early in television's rise, he became a panelist on *Quizzing the News*. He made frequent one-time appearances on many shows, including *Beulah*. He was Professor Warren on both the radio and TV versions of *The Halls of Ivy*.

Bryan continued his roles on *The Great Gildersleeve* and *Fibber McGee and Molly* until their respective endings in 1954 and 1959. Though he had experienced no previous symptoms, he suffered a sudden heart attack and died on November 18, 1959, at the age of sixty.

## KEN CHRISTY (POLICE CHIEF DONALD GATES)

When he was born on November 23, 1894, the name on his birth certificate was Robert Kenneth Christy. When he found his way into radio and films, he did as many actors did and shortened it to the more easily remembered Ken Christy. It apparently worked with the people who hired actors, but most radio listeners and moviegoers would be unlikely to recognize the name or be able to identify the face.

Christy performed on dozens of radio programs, but always in supporting or incidental roles. Between 1940 and 1962, he appeared in 144 films and television programs, but again in supporting roles, sometimes uncredited.

He broke into radio in the early 1930s and worked in that medium for three decades until it was overshadowed by television. He had assorted roles on numerous soap operas. Ready and willing to do comedy or serious drama, he was heard on *A Day in the Life of Dennis Day*, *Jack Armstrong*, *The Alan Young Show*, *Gangbusters*, and *The Saint*. Juvenile listeners heard him on *Little Orphan Annie* and *Smilin' Ed McConnell's Buster Brown Gang*. For one season he was Daddy's boss, Mr. Weemish, on the *Baby Snooks* show.

In 1940, Christy made his film debut in a series of comedy shorts and a small part in *Dr. Kildare Goes Home*. He subsequently was in such diverse pictures as *Foreign Correspondent*, *Tarzan's New York Adventure*, *A Place in the Sun*, *Cheaper By the Dozen* and *Abbott and Costello Go to Mars*. In his dozens of film roles, he played every type of lawman, from an Old West sheriff to a modern-day cop. In *Sunset Blvd.*, he was the homicide detective questioning Norma Desmond. Joking about this typecasting, he once said, "I'd give anything to stop making arrests and just once be the guy who commits the crime."

On television, he played assorted roles on *Death Valley Days*, *Meet Corliss Archer*, *I Love Lucy*, *Dragnet*, *Wagon Train*, *General Electric Theater*, *My Three Sons* and *M Squad*.

On *Gildersleeve*, he was again obliged to play a lawman, but as Chief Gates he was an easygoing fellow seen in his off-duty hours, mostly with the Jolly Boys, and often as the peacemaker.

Christy was sixty-seven years old when he died in Hollywood on July 23, 1962.

## RICHARD CRENNA (WALTER "BRONCO" THOMPSON)

Born November 30, 1926, Richard Donald Crenna was the only child of Domenick and Edith Crenna. His father was a pharmacist. His mother managed a small Los Angeles hotel, where the family resided.

When Richard was just eleven years old, one of his teachers steered him to an audition at nearby station KFI. That resulted in his first radio role as a not-too-bright kid who did everything wrong on *Boy Scout Jamboree*. He made sporadic appearances in various roles until 1948.

Bitten by the acting bug, he found openings for small parts on numerous programs, even as he earned high school letters in track and basketball. After graduation, he enrolled at the University of Southern California and majored in theater arts.

Crenna probably was first really noticed by radio listeners in

1946, when he took on the role of Oogie Pringle, the boyfriend of Judy Foster (Louise Erickson), on *A Date with Judy*. Judy was a teenager who spent much of her time chatting about boys on the phone with her girlfriends. When he came to pick her up for a date, Oogie would break off in mid-greeting to declare: "Boy, Judy, do you look *sna-a-zzy*!"

Richard had perfected the sound of a teenage boy whose voice had not quite changed. He would later put it to use on the *Our Miss Brooks* program. There he played Walter Denton, a student at Madison High School, where Miss Brooks (Eve Arden) taught and Principal Osgood Conklin (Gale Gordon) ruled with an iron hand.

Walter was a whiz on the basketball court, but struggled to maintain passing grades. As the heartthrob of Conklin's daughter, Harriet, he prompted many a parental outburst, at which Gordon excelled. When the show moved to television in 1952, Crenna remained in the cast and managed to pass himself off as a teenager.

Richard dropped the adenoidal voice when he joined the *Gildersleeve* cast as Walter J. Thompson, nicknamed Bronco. It was one of his last ongoing radio roles.

As radio roles became scarce, he moved smoothly into television and films. He had incidental roles on *I Love Lucy*, *The Millionaire*, the Western series *Cheyenne* and *Father Knows Best*. He was Senator James Slattery in the CBS drama series *Slattery's People* and Luke McCoy in the comedy series *The Real McCoys*.

Crenna appeared in a number of Western films, including *The Man Called Noon* and *Breakheart Pass*. He co-starred with Steve McQueen in *The Sand Pebbles*. During the 1980s, he became familiar as Colonel Trautman in the first three of Sylvester Stallone's *Rambo* pictures.

He was seventy-six years old and had appeared in more than seventy films when he died of heart failure on January 17, 2003.

## LURENE TUTTLE (MARJORIE FORRESTER, 1941–1944)

Born in Indiana on August 19, 1907, Lurene Tuttle soon moved with her family to Glendale, Arizona. Her father was a former vaudeville performer. With his encouragement, she studied acting as a child and was soon noticed for her scene-stealing comic antics.

When she was fifteen, her family moved to Monrovia, California. She began taking drama lessons at the Pasadena Playhouse and appearing in many of their productions. She then became a member of the vaudeville troupe Murphy's Comedians. That kept her busy and broadened her dramatic range through the 1920s and well into the 1930s.

Radio was by then providing a whole new stage for performers and required no traveling. In 1936, she auditioned for a role on *Hollywood Hotel* with Dick Powell and won a three-year contract. She never looked back.

In the early years, radio performers who were not big-name stars received shamefully low wages. Lurene and fellow *Hollywood Hotel* cast member Frank Nelson became active members of a union group that became the American Federation of Television and Radio Artists (AFTRA). Lurene later was the first female president of the organization's Hollywood unit.

She was heard frequently on more than one hundred programs, including *Duffy's Tavern*, *Dr. Christian*, *One Man's Family*, *Dragnet*, *The Whistler* and *Suspense*. She was a regular cast member in supporting roles on *Lux Radio Theatre*. On *The Red Skelton Show*, she played Daisy June, the girlfriend of Clem Kadiddlehopper, and the mother of Junior, "the mean widdle kid." She was Howard Duff's secretary Effie on *The Adventures of Sam Spade* and played almost every other female role on the series.

When she took on the role of Marjorie on *The Great Gildersleeve*, she was a regular or recurring cast member on half a dozen other programs. At times she was appearing on as many as fifteen programs per week. She was dubbed "First Lady of Radio" and one newspaper columnist called her "quite possibly the most-heard woman in America."

As radio roles disappeared, Lurene made a smooth transition to television. She filled more than one hundred roles between 1950 and the mid-1980s, including a dozen in made-for-television movies. Too mature to play a teen on TV, she was often a wife, mother or working woman. In November, 1953, she became Lavinia (Vinnie) Day, wife of Clarence Day, Sr., on the television series adaptation of *Life with Father*. After the show was discontinued in July, 1955, she and co-star Leon Ames went on the road in a stage production of the original play.

Her guest appearances included *Hazel*, *Leave It to Beaver*,

*General Electric Theater, Fantasy Island, I Dream of Jeannie, Murder, She Wrote* and many more. She was defended multiple times by Perry Mason, although once she was the murderess.

She took a hankering to Westerns and was seen on *Colt .45, Little House on the Prairie, Bonanza, Gunsmoke* and others.

Lurene had her film debut in 1947's *Heaven Only Knows*. Although never graced with a starring role, she appeared in forty-four films, including supporting roles in *Mr. Blandings Builds His Dream House* (with Cary Grant), *Don't Bother to Knock* (Marilyn Monroe), *Goodbye, My Fancy* (Joan Crawford), *The Glass Slipper* (Leslie Caron) and others. If you look sharply, you can see her as the sheriff's wife in Alfred Hitchcock's classic *Psycho*.

As far back as the 1940s, Lurene served as a drama and diction coach for many performers. She found great satisfaction in that work and continued with it long after her radio days. In an interview with old-time radio historian Chuck Schaden, she explained that on radio "we had to work with an all-physical person." By using your voice, she explained, "you could conjure up a person who lives and breathes…and is anything you wanted to be."

At the age of seventy-eight, Lurene Tuttle succumbed to cancer at her Encino home on May 28, 1986.

## LOUISE ERICKSON (MARJORIE FORRESTER, 1944 - 1948)

Born on February 28, 1928, Louise Erickson began her acting career in a royal fashion. When she was but seven years old, and her family moved from Oakland, California, to Hollywood, she auditioned for and was chosen to play a fairy princess on a kids' program called *Uncle Whoa Bill*. She soon joined a cast of young performers on the Mutual Broadcasting System's *Dramas of Youth*.

Her perky performances led to a network debut on *Dr. Christian* when she was only thirteen. She later appeared on *The Alan Young Show* (as Alan's girlfriend, Betty), *The Cavalcade of America* and other grown-up programs. In 1942, her career took a great leap forward when she landed a plum role as Mitzi, the best friend of Judy Foster, on *A Date with Judy*.

The show had begun as a 1941 summer replacement for *The Bob Hope Show* and proved so popular that it returned in various time slots into 1950. For Judy, initially played by Ann Gillis, an "absolute low" was to "not rate a date" for three nights running. Her only concerns in life were boys, school, boys, hairstyles, boys, makeup, boys, dating…and boys. Louise assumed the role in 1943 and was perfect as the teenager with an infectious giggle and given to outbursts of "Oh, dreeaaamy!" and "Sen-saysh!"

Louise had ample opportunity to demonstrate her wider range of acting on such programs as *The Lady Esther Screen Guild Theatre*, *The Phil Harris-Alice Faye Show*, *The Adventures of the Saint* and *The Adventures of Ozzie and Harriet*. She was Chester A. Riley's eldest daughter, Babs, on *The Life of Riley*.

Erickson either did not seek or did not attract much attention in Hollywood. She did have a few supporting roles in pictures, including 1944's *Meet Miss Bobby Socks* and the musical comedy *Rosie the Riveter*. When MGM did a screen version of *A Date with Judy*, they elected to star Jane Powell. In the opinion of one reviewer, "…they should have stuck with the original."

In lieu of doing television, she moved to New York in the 1950s. After a small role on Broadway in *A Hole in the Head*, she abandoned acting to do some writing and accepted a position as a museum tour guide for handicapped children.

As Marjorie Forrester, Louise played a more mature teenager than Judy. Of her time on *The Great Gildersleeve*, she reminisced: "Of all the programs I did on radio, [it] is the one that still stands up today. The writing was superb, and Hal Peary was a comedic genius."

One of the last surviving performers from the Golden Age of Radio, Louise Erickson died March 18, 2019. She was ninety-one.

## MARY LEE ROBB (MARJORIE FORRESTER, 1948 - 1954)

Unlike many of her radio peers, Mary Lee Robb did not evidence any early yearning to perform. Born February 15, 1926, in Streator, Illinois, she soon moved with her family to Chicago, where her father was an executive at NBC. Though she and her mother sometimes visited the studio, Mary Lee led a normal young girl's life through her grade school years.

In 1939, the family moved to Los Angeles. There she graduated from University High School and attended UCLA. Not until 1947 did she make her radio debut, and then by a fortunate happenstance. A small role on *Lum and Abner* needed to be filled. Mary Lee was there (and her father was an exec). Would she like to give it a try? She agreed, and she did just fine with her two lines: "I do," and "Don't cry, Papa."

It wasn't exactly *A Star Is Born*, but it led to other appearances. She soon was performing with star Gordon MacRae on *The Railroad Hour*. She ranged from Western adventures on *Red Ryder* to comedy on *The Penny Singleton Show*, to modern-day crime stories on *This Is Your FBI*. She was a sound effects performer of sorts on the *Baby Snooks* series. She voiced the crying of Snooks' baby brother, Robespierre. Other than her time on the *Gildersleeve* program, her longest running role was that of Emily Vanderlip, a young next-door neighbor on *Burns and Allen*.

Another small incident led to her role as Marjorie on *The Great Gildersleeve*. Mary Lee was at a rehearsal expecting to read a couple of lines. Louise Erickson, the current Marjorie, was delayed, and Mary Lee offered to read her lines. Her performance made a lasting impression. Time passed, Louise Erickson moved on, and Mary Lee was offered the role. She filled it nicely until 1954, when the character ceased appearing.

Mary Lee's first marriage, which ended in divorce, had produced a son, Robb, and a daughter, Alexandra. After *Gildersleeve*, she retired from performing to rear her children. In 1983, she married William H. Cline. That marriage lasted until her death on August 28, 2006, at age eighty.

## RICHARD LEGRAND (RICHARD QUINCY PEAVEY)

Richard LeGrand was born August 29, 1882, and spent his youth with his family in their home near Portland, Oregon. When he was sixteen, an adventurous urge led him to become a sailor. For three years he enjoyed visiting such destinations as England, Ireland and parts of the Orient.

When he was nineteen, he found himself unemployed in New York City. A sign at the Bijou Theatre said they were looking for a stagehand. He applied and got the job. The pay was a pittance, but when you're broke and hungry, any port in a storm.

Richard's job was to operate an artificial snow machine. His acting career began when he was recruited to fill a small role as a butler. That led to some other parts that required a few more lines and more stage time.

Thinking this was not a bad way to earn a living, he returned to Oregon for a home visit and then joined the Dillon and King repertory company. He developed a skill for doing a variety of voices, and for the next five years he found theater work in dramas, musical comedies, tent shows and vaudeville.

In 1928, radio was still in its infancy and Richard was in San Francisco. There he made his on-air debut as announcer for *The Spotlight Revue*. The following year, he portrayed Professor Knicklebine on a program called *School Days*. Using a Swedish accent, he worked with a female trio on one of radio's first regularly sponsored programs, *Ole and the Girls*. Many years later, he put the same voice to work on *Fibber McGee and Molly*. He played Ole, janitor at the Elks Club lodge, whose signature line was, "I'm yust donatin' my time." He was heard on *One Man's Family*, *I Love a Mystery* and other continuing dramas. During the last year of the *Phil Harris-Alice Faye Show*, he played Phil's father.

No doubt Richard is best remembered as the quiet, patient drugstore owner, Peavey, on the *Gildersleeve* show, where he appeared for most of the program's run. In 1951, his fiftieth year as a performer, the National Association of Retail Druggists named him "America's Favorite Neighborhood Druggist."

When he was financially secure, some remnant of his seagoing urge led LeGrand to purchase a small yacht. Mary Lee Robb recalled that he enjoyed hosting onboard parties for the *Gildersleeve* cast. When it got late, he would announce: "Party's over. Cast off!"

Richard made a few screen appearances, including his Peavey role in three of the *Gildersleeve* films. In 1943's *Gildersleeve on Broadway*, his part almost overshadowed that of the presumed star, Harold Peary.

Richard died June 29, 1963, at the age of eighty-one.

## SHIRLEY MITCHELL (LEILA RANSOM)

Shirley Mitchell was born in Toledo, Ohio, on November 4, 1926. As a youngster, she demonstrated a penchant for performing in local amateur shows. When just thirteen, she auditioned at Detroit station WXYZ and won a role on *The Lone Ranger*.

A dutiful daughter, she finished high school and attended college, but was soon working as an apprentice at the Cleveland Playhouse. Her parents were doubtful when she headed to Chicago to seek work on radio, but she promised to return and become a school teacher if she failed. Within two weeks she appeared on *The First Nighter* as a Southern belle (a role she would later play for laughs on *Gildersleeve*). She followed that with appearances on some soap operas, including *Road of Life* and *The Story of Mary Marlin*.

She moved to Los Angeles and found recurring roles on *The Jack Carson Show* and *The Sealtest Village Store*, with Joan Davis and Jack Haley. She was Honeybee Gillis on *The Life of Riley* with William Bendix and the secretary, Helen, on *The Bill Goodwin Show*. During World War II, she was Alice Darling, a defense plant worker rooming at the home of *Fibber McGee and Molly*.

Mitchell enjoyed a starring role as Kitty Archer on the comedy detective series *McGarry and His Mouse*. An incidental appearance as a Red Cross nurse in 1942 led to her recurring role as the oh-so-Southern belle Leila Ransom on *Gildersleeve* in 1943.

Whether due to a lack of interest or for want of a good agent, her work in films was minimal. She did appear in several films during the 1940s and 1950s, but her roles were not memorable.

Her work on television covered more territory. She appeared in several episodes of *I Love Lucy* and *Perry Mason*. She was the recurring character Janet Colton on *Pete and Gladys*. She was neighbor Marge Thornton on *Please Don't Eat the Daisies* and Cousin Mae on *Petticoat Junction*.

During her radio years, she took some time off to marry and live with her surgeon husband in New York City. The marriage produced a son, Scott, and a daughter, Brooke. In her later years, she filled some of her time doing voice-over work.

Shirley Mitchell died of heart failure on November 11, 2013, at the age of ninety-four.

## LILLIAN RANDOLPH (BIRDIE LEE COGGINS)

Lillian Randolph, born December 14, 1898, was the daughter of a preacher and a schoolteacher. She made her first public performance at the age of four. At her father's Methodist church in a suburb of Pittsburgh, Pennsylvania, she sang a gospel song, accompanied on the piano by her older sister, Amanda. Before long, the duo was performing frequently in and around their area.

Both sisters had aspirations of singing professionally. While Lillian was still in her mid-teens, Amanda began singing with a small group. Lillian got her chance with a little devious help from her sister.

A band in Cincinnati was looking for a female singer. Lillian wanted to audition, but was too nervous. Her sister used her name, did the singing, and was hired. Then Amanda told her, "Now you go sing." The girls looked and sounded alike. Lillian sang with the band for two summers and no one ever noticed that she was a bit younger.

A few gigs elsewhere led to her first opportunity to sing on radio at Cleveland station WTAM. Next she went to Detroit station WXYZ, where *The Lone Ranger* originated. She was to audition as part of a group, but no one else showed up. Station owner George W. Trendle took her on anyway, initially to do a skit with comedian Billy Mitchell.

In preparation for the show, she was given lessons by a voice coach on speaking with what was the stereotypical perception of a black person's dialect. Trendle paid her $30 a week while she trained, a tidy sum then. When she was deemed ready, she and Billy went on the air in a program called *Lulu and Leander*. They each did five voices.

Years later, Lillian laughed about the preposterous notion of having to learn how to speak like a "colored woman," but she observed that it proved profitable. She filled a number of other small roles while in Detroit.

For an ambitious young performer, the West Coast offered more opportunities than Detroit. In 1936, she moved to Los Angeles. She visited many agencies and was often called upon when they needed someone to play such black characters as a maid, a cook, or a nanny. In between radio parts, she did some cabaret singing.

For a time, radio roles were intermittent and she lived on a very tight budget. Ironically, her breakthrough in 1940 came with her appearance on Al Jolson's show. Jolson was famous for his performances singing in blackface. Soon she began appearing on shows with Al Pearce, Billie Burke and others. She was Madame Queen on *Amos 'n' Andy* and Mrs. Watson on *Baby Snooks*. During part of its tenure, she was the star of the *Beulah* program.

No doubt her most memorable radio role was that of Birdie Lee Coggins on *The Great Gildersleeve*. She was heard on the first program and was there until the last. When she sang "Were You There?" on the program, it resulted in an invitation to record an album of gospel songs. That was a joy for her to perform.

Lillian liked to tell the story of how she came to win the role of Birdie. She was late to the auditions. Hurrying into the building, she dashed down the hall and charged through the studio door. The floor was smooth and slick. She slid all across the room and kept from falling only by grabbing hold of the stand-up microphone. A group of women were seated nearby after having given their auditions. They watched with open mouths, as did producer Cecil Underwood, the men in the control room and the other studio crew. Lillian just clung to the microphone and burst out laughing.

After everyone breathed a sigh of relief, she was handed a script. She got through the audition smoothly. When she was done, Underwood nodded and said to the crew, "This is the gal we want." It proved to be a wise choice. Lillian was a key member of the program's cast for its entire run. Of cast and crew, she later remembered: "Oh, they were the nicest people. Harold Peary was great to work with."

*Gildersleeve* provided Lillian with steady employment for its duration, but she found time to fill other prominent roles. From 1943 through 1955, she was Madam Queen on the popular and long-running *Amos 'n' Andy* show. When Hattie McDaniel, star of *The Beulah Show*, took ill, Lillian assumed the role for the 1951-1952 season. She then turned it over to her big sister, Amanda.

Lillian broke into films with a small part in 1938's *Life Goes On*. Over the next forty years, she appeared in dozens of films, including *Little Men* (1940), *Heaven Can Wait* (1943), *Up in Arms* (1944), *The Bachelor and the Bobby-Soxer* (1947), *That's My Boy* (1951),

*Once Is Not Enough* (1975) and *The Onion Field* (1979). She also appeared, as Birdie, in four *Gildersleeve* films. She was the fearsome voice of big-footed Mammy in the *Tom and Jerry* cartoons.

When radio faded out, she reprised her Madame Queen persona on the *Amos 'n' Andy* television show. She was Bill Cosby's mother on *The Bill Cosby Show* and she made assorted appearances on *Sanford and Son* and *The Jeffersons*. She was a slave named Sister Sara in 1977's acclaimed miniseries *Roots*.

Apart from her Birdie role on radio, Lillian probably is best remembered as the Bailey family's lovable maid, Annie, in *It's a Wonderful Life*, the film that has become a holiday television classic.

Lillian Randolph died of cancer on September 12, 1980, at the age of eighty-one. She was buried next to her sister Amanda at Forest Lawn Memorial Park in Hollywood Hills.

## EARLE ROSS (JUDGE HORACE HOOKER)

If his parents had their wish, Earle Ross would have been a Methodist minister. Born in Chicago, March 29, 1888, he was groomed for his actual career by his early singing in the boys' choir. One day his voice cracked and he was speechless for several days. When he recovered, his vocal chords had undergone a strange transformation. He sounded not just mature, but almost like an old man.

In high school, Earle became interested in the drama group, where he was chosen for several roles as a villain or an old man thanks to his voice. His parents were no doubt gratified when he worked with Colonel Bill Selig on the 1908 film *The Holy Cross*.

Making up with enthusiasm for what he lacked in experience, he ventured to the East Coast in 1912 and found work in several Broadway productions. In one melodrama, he played three roles and was paid extra for serving as stage manager.

The Great Depression and the rise of radio may have been the incentives for Earle to become a pioneer in the new medium. He soon was starring in a continuing drama called *Inspector Post* and hosting his own program, *The Earle Ross Theater of the Air*.

Whether he was considering the possibility of a film career or just seeking a warmer climate, Ross relocated to Hollywood in the mid-1930s. Neither his looks nor his voice favored him for leading man roles. Nevertheless, he landed supporting roles in *The Courageous Dr. Christian* and *A Date with the Falcon*. Casting directors evidently found his looks and voice suitable for Western parts. In one year alone, he appeared in four: *Cavalry*, *The Gun Ranger*, *Stormy Trails*, and *Riders of the Whistling Skull*.

It was in radio, however, that he found his niche. Back in Chicago during the early 1940s, he appeared on such shows as *Lights Out* and *The Theater of Famous Radio Players*. By the mid-1940s, he was back on the West Coast and enjoying a busy schedule on numerous programs. He made frequent appearances on *The Railroad Hour*, *Lux Radio Theatre*, *The Cavalcade of America*, *Hallmark Playhouse* and *Favorite Story*. He had incidental or recurring roles on *The Mel Blanc Show*, *Michael Shayne, Detective*, *The Billie Burke Show* and others. On *Meet Millie*, he played J. R. Boone, Sr., who was not enthused about his secretary Millie's crush on his son, Johnny. Ross's gruff voice was perfect for his periodic comic remarks meant to discourage any romance. Lest his Western casting get rusty, he also appeared on *The Roy Rogers Show*. Though he never really made the transition to television, he did put his Western persona to use on *The Adventures of Wild Bill Hickok*.

No doubt his most memorable role, however, was that of the crusty Judge Horace Hooker, the friendly antagonist of Throckmorton P. Gildersleeve. His sly, cackling laugh was a perfect counterpoint to the self-satisfied chuckle or "dirty laugh" of the great man.

Earle Ross died of cancer in North Hollywood, California, on May 21, 1961. He was seventy-three.

## WALTER TETLEY (LEROY FORRESTER)

Walter Campbell Tetley had a unique career in radio. He was born in New York City on June 2, 1915. His mother, Jessie, was born in Scotland and claimed she could trace her ancestry back to William the Conqueror.

When Walter was but a toddler, Jessie began singing songs of her homeland to him and he was quick to pick them up. As he grew to preschool age, he frequently listened to his mother's collection of recordings by the famous Scottish entertainer Sir Harry Lauder. To his mother's great pleasure, he proved himself a born entertainer, singing the songs in a precise imitation.

Adept at dressmaking, Jessie made Walter a kilt and rented a miniature set of bagpipes. He did his impersonation at a meeting of the Daughters of Scotia and was a sensation. With Jessie as his agent, Walter began performing at church and civic events throughout New York, New Jersey and Pennsylvania. He was billed as Wee Sir Harry Lauder and for a time toured with the Keith-Orpheum vaudeville circuit.

Walter Tetley as "Wee Sir Harry Lauder"

Due to what was later diagnosed as a hormonal disorder, Walter did not grow at the normal rate. When he was well into his teens, he was still much shorter than his peers and he never experienced the adolescent change of voice. As she continued to arrange appearances for him, his mother passed him off as being half his real age.

In 1929, when Walter was fourteen, his mother took him to

NBC's New York City studios. He auditioned as a child and was chosen to appear on a popular Sunday morning program, *The Children's Hour*. His Harry Lauder impersonation again earned raves and he was called back to appear on a program called *The Lady Next Door*. The lady was Marge Tucker, hostess of a program that featured children and was aimed at a junior audience.

After several appearances on the program, Walter was signed to a contract with NBC. He was hailed as the youngest performer ever to have a network contract. In 1931, he was grabbed coming off an elevator, rushed into an NBC studio and handed a script to replace a young actor who had taken sick. With no rehearsal, he read his lines perfectly and with the appropriate emotion. The result was a leading role in a series called *Raising Junior*.

Over the next couple of years, he was heard on numerous programs now long forgotten and others such as *The March of Time* and *Death Valley Days*. He played Tigger in an adaptation of *Winnie the Pooh* and was Tip in a series based on *The Wizard of Oz*.

In 1935, Fred Allen called on Walter to play a sassy kid who showed up from time to time in Allen's Alley. He was also heard, sassy or not, in occasional guest roles with Jack Benny, Joe Penner and Burns and Allen. He also became a regular cast member on *The Adventures of Bobby Benson* playing a Scottish boy (typecasting?).

At the urging of Fred Allen, Walter moved to the West Coast in 1937 and was given a small part in a film Fred was doing. He began auditioning at various studios and played a Scottish lad (again) in 1938's *Lord Jeff*. He followed that with a part in Gene Autry's Western *Prairie Moon*. The next year he appeared in five films. He was a chimney sweep in *Tower of London* with Boris Karloff and did a brief comic bit with W. C. Fields in *You Can't Cheat an Honest*

*Man*. He had a rare featured role in *They Shall Have Music* with concert violinist Jascha Heifetz.

Walter did grow a few inches in his teens, but he remained shorter than most of his schoolmates. After he turned twenty-one, he was treated by a urologist. Slowly, over a period of years, he grew to almost six feet tall. His voice scarcely changed, however. Though it was no longer childlike, he still sounded like a boy in his early teens.

In February, 1939, Walter was called on for an incidental appearance on *Fibber McGee and Molly*. There he met and worked with Hal Peary for the first time. Peary remembered him later when the cast of *The Great Gildersleeve* was being assembled.

Tetley continued filling many film roles through the 1940s, albeit mostly small parts. He was cast more than once as a bellhop, including the Abbott and Costello comedy *Who Done It?* One of his last screen appearances was with comedian Bert Gordon, known as The Mad Russian, in 1945's *How DOooo You Do!!!*

Walter's radio renown was cemented with his selection to play Leroy on *The Great Gildersleeve*. He was heard on the first episode and prevailed until the last. He missed out only on the brief television version because he had outgrown the twelve- or thirteen-year-old he portrayed on radio.

Other than Leroy Forrester, Tetley's best remembered radio role surely is that of grocery delivery boy Julius Abbruzio on *The Phil Harris-Alice Faye Show*. Walter joined the cast in 1948 and was an instant hit.

Julius' voice was similar to that of Leroy's, but had an abrasive tone that Tetley spiked with a distinct touch of Brooklyn accent. Sounding a bit like a Dead End Kid, he used such phrases as "me mudda" or "ya wanna?" He had a scarcely concealed crush on Alice. He always addressed her as "Miss Faye" and often wondered aloud how such a swell lady could be married to such a dunce as Phil.

His opinion of Phil and his pal Frankie Remley was summarized in his frequent greeting to them: "What are youse two geniuses up to today?" Phil and Frankie were alternately out to put Julius down in some fashion or seeking his advice or assistance with some mess into which they had gotten themselves.

Julius' incredulous response to Phil and Frankie's dilemmas led him to demand: "Are you kiddin'?" Or: "Get outta here!" When the twosome's schemes really strained his credulity, it prompted outbursts of: "Wait'll my old man hears about this!" Or: "You want I should call the cops?!?" These all became catchphrases that the audience anticipated hearing from Julius.

Walter was on the show until it ended in 1954. Even when Tetley was nearing forty, Phil would introduce him during audience warm-ups as "the kid who steals the show every week."

Television was not for Tetley, but after radio he found a new niche in voice-over work. Those who remember the *Rocky and His Friends* television cartoon series heard him as Sherman, the nerdy, bespectacled boy companion of time-traveling dog genius Mr. Peabody. He voiced ninety-one episodes of *Peabody's Improbable History*. In another humorous historical mode, he was heard on the recorded satirical masterpiece *Stan Freberg Presents the United States of America*.

In 1973, when Rod Serling dared to attempt a radio revival with his *Zero Hour* series, Walter made his last appearance in an episode called "Princess Stakes Murder." He was by then doing limited voice-over work and confined to a wheelchair. In 1971, he was riding a motorcycle and was struck by a motorist who ran a red light. He spent almost a year in hospital and never fully recovered.

In the 1940s, once he had established himself in Hollywood and was doing well financially, he bought a house in Van Nuys and brought his parents out to live with him. It was their home for the remainder of their lives.

Despite his Scottish lineage, however, Walter was not given to frugality and had little in the way of savings or investments. After his accident, he lost the house and spent his last few years in a trailer. The Encino trailer park was operated by a friend, and it's believed that Walter may have been living there rent-free.

On June 17, 1975, Walter Tetley was admitted to Beverly Manor Convalescent Hospital in Canoga Park, California. It was there that he died on September 7, 1975, at the age of sixty.

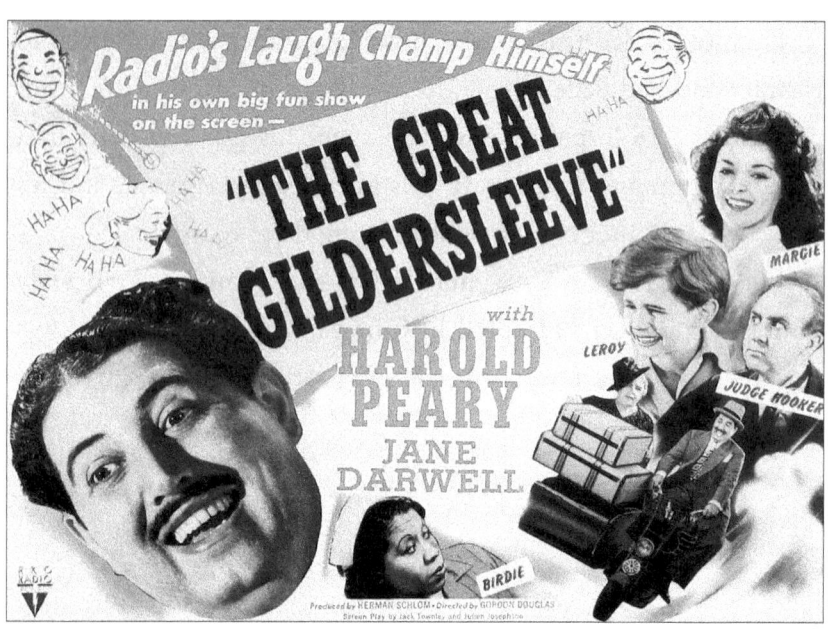

# GILDERSLEEVE ON THE BIG SCREEN

EVEN BEFORE HE had his own program, Throckmorton P. Gildersleeve was popular enough that he began appearing in the movies, albeit in minor roles. He made his screen debut in the 1940 Paramount film *Comin' Round the Mountain*, starring comedian Bob Burns. As Mayor Gildersleeve, he is running for reelection and has stiff competition from a candidate promoted by Bob. He is joined in the countrified antics by Una Merkel, comedian Jerry Colonna, Don Wilson (Jack Benny's longtime announcer) and fellow *Fibber McGee and Molly* cast member Bill Thompson.

In 1941, still using the Gildersleeve name, he appeared in *Country Fair*, starring Eddie Foy, Jr. This time he has raised his sights and is running for an office for which he is even more unqualified—governor! Fortunately for the citizens of the state, he is not elected.

That same year, he joined Jim and Marian Jordan (Fibber and Molly McGee) in their first starring film, *Look Who's Laughing*. As a rather devious fellow who wants to build a factory in Wistful Vista, he is overshadowed by the McGees and co-stars Lucille Ball, ventriloquist Edgar Bergen, and Bergen's wooden pal, Charlie McCarthy.

The Jordans followed that film with 1942's *Here We Go Again*. Fibber and Molly plan a second honeymoon for their 20th anniversary. Edgar Bergen returns, and this time brings along both Charlie and his hayseed companion, Mortimer Snerd. Gale Gordon appears as Mollie's long-ago beau, Otis Cadwalader, and Isabel Randolph as Abigail Uppington. Gildersleeve is on hand, but he tends to get lost in the hubbub of multiple comic plot twists that include Bergen and McCarthy's run-in with some Indians.

No need to feel sorry for Peary, though. By this time, RKO Radio Pictures was prompted to capitalize upon the popularity of the *Gildersleeve* radio program by producing what would be the first of four films starring Harold Peary. Released in 1942, it was titled simply *The Great Gildersleeve*. Judge Horace Hooker's sister, Amelia, is husband hunting, and a misunderstanding leads her to believe that she is engaged to Throckmorton P. Gildersleeve. Niece Marjorie and nephew Leroy concoct a wild scheme that results in a slapstick rescue.

In *Gildersleeve's Bad Day* (1943), our hero is on a jury that will be hearing the trial of a gangster named Louie. Louie's gang decides that the best way to get their boss off is to "persuade" one juror to vote for acquittal. They pick Gildy. What follows is a convoluted farce that critics panned but probably was enjoyed by loyal fans.

*Gildersleeve on Broadway* (also 1943) finds Throckmorton on his way to New York City on a rescue mission. A drug supply company is about to go out of business, which may force Gildy's friend, Peavey, to close his drugstore. The company's president turns out to be a lonely woman who finds Gildersleeve attractive. A misunderstanding leads her to believe that they are engaged. Gildersleeve crashes a druggists' convention that's being held at his hotel and gets a contract signed that will keep Peavey in business. Peavey, learning of Gildy's unintended engagement, comes to the rescue by showing up dressed as "Mrs. Gildersleeve." Walter Tetley makes a brief appearance as (guess what?) a bellhop.

In *Gildersleeve's Ghost* (1944), Gildy has yet to learn his lesson and is again running for office. This time he hopes to become police commissioner. Two of his deceased relatives, Jonathan Q. Gildersleeve and Randolph Q. Gildersleeve, rise from their graves and seek to give him some spooky support. Much of the film is taken up by a side plot that involves a lot of monkey business. Leroy tries to win over animal lovers for his uncle by dressing up in a gorilla costume while a real escaped gorilla is on the loose. Use your imagination. Gildersleeve fans probably enjoyed the film. Reviewers were mostly in agreement, panning it. Harold Peary enjoyed it because he got to play three roles.

Because his physical appearance did not match the character he portrayed on radio, Walter Tetley did not play Leroy in any of the Gildersleeve films. That role was filled by a lad named Freddie Mercer. Marjorie Forrester was played by Nancy Gates in the first two films and by Margaret Landry and Margie Stewart respectively in the last two.

Charles Arnt took up the role of Judge Horace Hooker in the first two films.

Richard LeGrand was Peavey in all but the first film. In *Gildersleeve on Broadway* his role was such as to be rated as a co-star. In *Gildersleeve's Bad Day*, Ken Christy appeared, not as Summerfield's police chief, but as a court bailiff. Lillian Randolph tagged along in all four films as the lovable and irrepressible Birdie Lee Coggins.

In 1942, Harold Peary also appeared in *Seven Days' Leave*, a comedy starring Victor Mature and Lucille Ball. Private Johnny Grey (Mature) learns that he is the heir to a small fortune. Peary has a supporting role as the attorney representing his great-grandfather's estate, who explains the unwelcome conditions under which he will qualify. Because NBC insisted upon it, the character is named Throckmorton P. Gildersleeve. Any resemblance to the Summerfield water commissioner is purely coincidental.

# IN CONCLUSION

THROCKMORTON P. GILDERSLEEVE was created by the wickedly witty mind of Don Quinn and brought to life by the vivid imagination and talent of Harold Peary. Peary's ability to express Gildy's moods and emotions via his vocal intonations was something akin to verbal body language.

Because Gildy originated as a neighbor of the McGees, *The Great Gildersleeve* will always be recognized by old-time radio aficionados as radio's first spin-off program in the comedy category. More than that, however, it was a program that drew its humor from a gentle combination of human frailties and nonsensical farce.

Recurring characters were never so overdone as to be unbelievable. Most of them were just imperfect enough that they might remind listeners of some relative or friend who tended to be a bit... well, you know. Somehow you knew that, whatever nonsense was occurring, everything would be all right by show's end, and a few laughs were had along the way.

*The Great Gildersleeve* was heard from August, 1941, until March, 1957, a respectable run, if not a record. Fortunately, many of the original electronic transcriptions (16-inch vinyl recordings) and later reel-to-reel tapes have been preserved by individual collectors and such organizations as Chicago's Museum of Broadcast

Communications. Deemed to be in the public domain, most have become available to old-time radio fans, first on cassette tapes and later on audio discs. Many can be tuned in on various free Internet sites. Fans in some areas are even blessed with local radio programs such as *Those Were the Days*, heard in the Chicago metropolitan area, that air the old shows, complete with commercials.

As younger generations "discover" old-time radio, *Gildersleeve* and countless other programs from radio's golden age will continue to be enjoyed. If they were still with us, Harold Peary would no doubt express his satisfaction with a dirty laugh, while Don Quinn would look and see that it is good.

# ACKNOWLEDGEMENTS

IN SPITE OF my enthusiasm and the enjoyment I experienced in putting this book together, it would have been a less satisfying project were it not for a number of people who contributed to its completion. Thanks are due to all.

After the publication of my *Old-Time Radio's Comedy Couples*, it was publisher Ben Ohmart who suggested that my next subject might be Gildersleeve.

The prolific Martin Grams, Jr., author of numerous books on the subject of old-time radio, found time in his busy schedule to compose an insightful foreword.

Old-time radio broadcaster and historian Chuck Schaden cleared up some grey areas for me and offered a few insights. Jim Cox, author of numerous books about programs and performers of radio's golden age, filled in some gaps, as did Dave Goldin, proprietor of the impressively cataloged website RadioGOLDINdex.com.

With the exception of the big stars, the faces of most *Gildersleeve* performers were unknown to audiences of the marvelous medium that was radio. So, a work such as this would be incomplete without pictures to put faces to names. Steve Darnall, editor/publisher of the quarterly *Nostalgia Digest* magazine, supplied a swell *Fibber*

*McGee* cast photo from the period when Harold Peary was a regular. From Chuck Schaden's *Speaking of Radio* website came photos of several *Gildersleeve* cast members. With one exception, all the rest were supplied by Ben Ohmart from the BearManor Media photo collection.

Despite his many film and radio roles, Ken Christy proved elusive. None of my usual sources could come up with a photo of him. I reached out to the Library of Congress, where a bountiful photo collection covers much of our history, including theater and arts. Jonathan Eaker and Rosemary Hayes searched through their respective department files, but both came up empty.

Then Rosemary suggested that I try contacting the Margaret Herrick Library in Beverly Hills, California. I did, and reference librarian Genevieve Maxwell came to my rescue. She located a fine photo of Christy from the archives of the Hollywood Museum collection. Ken Christy, who played detectives and other lawmen in many films, would likely have nodded his approval of the search-and-find adventure.

Daughter Laurie McGuire reviewed my first draft and offered her professional editor's comments and suggestions for modifications. When I received the publisher's proof copy, she joined me in looking for anything that needed fixing. Good thing. She spotted a few things I missed.

Daughter Jennifer McGuire lent her tech-savvy skills to the preparation of my first draft and final submission to the publisher. Her know-how often rescues me from my klutzy computer dilemmas.

Darlene Swanson got my text neatly formatted to fit the pages and found suitable spots to insert all of the photos. Then she put her creative talent to work and produced a nifty (1940s word) front and back cover for the book.

My sincere thanks to all who helped bring this work to completion.

And last, but definitely not least, a special thanks to the love of my life, who periodically reminds me that housewives do not get to retire. As I disappear for hours in a back room, she ignores the click-clack of my computer, goes about keeping our household in order, and makes sure that I eat three healthy meals daily. Thank you, Joy.

# REFERENCES

*Don't Touch That Dial* by Fred MacDonald. Nelson-Hall Publishers, 1979.

*Heavenly Days* by Charles Stumpf and Tom Price. World of Yesteryear Publishers, 1987.

*Nostalgia Digest* magazine; various issues and articles.

*On the Air: The Encyclopedia of Old-Time Radio* by John Dunning. Oxford University Press, 1998.

*Raised on Radio* by Gerald Nachman. Pantheon Books, 1998.

*Speaking of Radio*, interviews by Chuck Schaden. Nostalgia Digest Press, 2003.

*The Great Radio Sitcoms* by Jim Cox. McFarland & Company, 2007.

*Walter Tetley: For Corn's Sake* by Ben Ohmart. BearManor Media, 2016.

# ABOUT THE AUTHOR

Dan McGuire is a longtime contributor to *Nostalgia Digest* magazine, where he was a featured columnist for ten years. His first book, *Now, When I Was a Kid . . .: Nostalgic Ramblings*, is a collection of some favorite articles about fun times growing up in an era when the parlor radio was a prime source of family entertainment. He sells the book at his online store: *www.backwhenbooks.com*.

His most recent book, *Old-Time Radio's Comedy Couples*, is available from BearManor Media. It recalls the lives and careers of five beloved twosomes (can you name them?) who were married both on their programs and in real life.

Dan and his wife, Joy, will soon be celebrating sixty years of togetherness. They still reside in the house where they reared their elder daughter Laurie and twins David and Jennifer.